D0870944

WITHDRAWN

Tales from
Many Cultures

Penny Cameron

Addison-Wesley Publishing Company
Reading, Massachusetts • Menlo Park, California
New York • Don Mills, Ontario • Wokingham, England
Amsterdam • Bonn • Sydney • Singapore • Tokyo
Madrid • San Juan • Paris • Seoul, Korea • Milan
Mexico City • Taipei, Taiwan

Tales from Many Cultures

A Publication of World Language Division

Acquisitions editor: Anne Boynton-Trigg
Development editor: Debbie Sistino
Production editor: Nik Winter
Text design: Pencil Point Studio
Cover design: Curt Belshe
Text art: Yao-Zen Liu

Library of Congress Cataloging in Publication Data

Tales from many cultures / [edited by] Penny Cameron
     p.   cm.
  Contents: The eagle and the snake—Bouki rents a horse—Anansi and the stories—A dinner of smells—The blue lady of Jagua Castle—The monkey's heart—The moon god of the Mayas—Pedro Animala sells a carrao bird—Truong-Chi and the princess—Weaving girl and the cowherd.
  ISBN 0-201-82521-X
  1. English language—Textbooks for foreign speakers. 2. Readers—Manners and customs. 3. Manners and customs—Fiction.
I. Cameron, Penny.
PE1128.T322 1995
428.6'4—dc20   94-37550
                                                  CIP

11 12 CRS 0504

Contents

Introduction to the Teacher

Tales from Many Cultures is a collection of ten folktales from around the world written for low-level students.

The text reflects the principles of the whole language approach, so reading is viewed as an active and recursive process. The student goes into, through, and beyond the text, and constructs meaning and gains understanding from the reading. Working *into* the text, the student is asked to contribute his or her prior knowledge and experience, and to develop a context for the story. This context includes map work, historical references, and personal interpretation of the illustrations, which help in the understanding of the story.

When the student works *through* the story, further interaction occurs. The text is highly contextualized, so students can actively discover the meanings of new words and phrases. The exercises after each reading are designed to encourage creative student participation, in pairs or groups. This work has beneficial social effects as students learn the advantages of cooperation, and helps students make personal connections with the text. Low-level students need repitition and reassurance. There is a core of repeated exercises (described in detail later). Finally, the exercises that go *beyond* the text invite students to expand on what is already known and to apply this new knowledge to their own lives.

The stories in *Tales from Many Cultures* come from around the world and were selected if they were likely to be well known to a large group of students. The wise Nasrudin was claimed by so many Middle Eastern students that in the end "A Dinner of Smells" is described as "a story from the Middle East" to avoid argument. "Weaving Girl" is known all over Asia, and Pedro Animala makes people laugh in many Latin and Central American countries. He is not a good role model, and he is certainly not representative of the people of his area. Neither is Bouki—but they are both amusing!

Traditional stories show us how social attitudes have changed. Traditional stories have heroes who reflect the attitudes of the times the stories were told, and we must respect their integrity and not revise them, although we may certainly comment on the changes we see. The stories endure because they still make good reading as we enter the third millennium. They all deserve telling, and their themes reappear wherever stories are told. I hope you and your class enjoy them as much as my students and I did.

BEFORE YOU READ

Encourage students to look very carefully at the pictures and check that they can name the persons and objects in the pictures. Ask the questions in the book and encourage discussion. Inevitably, some students will read ahead and will have the right answers to prediction questions. Acknowledge their effort and try to guide the rest of the students to foresee the events of the story. Students at beginner levels may find speculation confusing, so the story is outlined in the pictures. If it is appropriate for your class, put the students' suggestions on the board so you can refer to their predictions as you go along.

THE STORY

Read the story aloud, slowly, allowing a lot of processing time and giving vocal clues (like deep sighs or laughter) wherever appropriate. Your performance should not be subtle! Have the students read silently while you read. Tell the students that you will read the story at least twice. If you would like to check vocabulary before the students answer the questions, read the story a third time and ask students to identify words they still do not know at the third reading. Alternatively, you may tell the students to check unknown vocabulary themselves, either in groups in class or for homework.

THE EXERCISES AFTER EACH STORY

After each story you will find a core of exercises, repetitive and familiar, designed to reassure the students. These exercises lend themselves to group or pair work and are designed to meet the varying needs of the students in a beginner class. The core consists of:

Are You Listening?: A listening exercise to encourage careful reading and listening. A section of the story is printed in the Teacher's Notes at the back of the book, but some words and phrases have been changed. It is the students' task to tell you when you have "made a mistake."

What Did You Understand?: A cloze comprehension passage.

Work with Words: A fill-in-the-blank vocabulary exercise.

What Happened?: A modeled writing exercise. The correct response is easily derived from the question, e.g., "Is Pedro Animala a trickster or an honest man?"

These core exercises are useful in building the students' confidence, but may be limiting for the more advanced members of the class.

The remaining exercises are inspired by the stories themselves and include:

Comprehension: Sequencing, choosing the best summary of the story, correcting wrong statements, true/false exercises.

Show What It Means: Miming how we look and move under the influence of different situations and emotions.

Listening/Speaking: Listening for accuracy, speaking happily or sadly, imitating the teacher's voice, distinguishing between orders and requests.

Vocabulary: Choosing the word that doesn't belong, word grid, semantic map, opposites.

A game or Total Physical Response: Tic tac toe, various forms of Simon Says, Twenty Questions.

Syntax/Writing: Scrambled sentences, describing a picture, correcting errors in description of a picture, SEPARATETHEWORDS in which the students must divide with slashes (SEPARATE/THE/WORDS), retelling the story, choosing the most important part of the story, scrambled stories, expressing an opinion.

Beyond the Story: Information about the country the story comes from, surveys of attitudes and opinions, information about the students' countries.
Specific suggestions for each exercise are in the Teacher's Notes.

READING ALOUD

Reading aloud is suggested here and *not* in the body of the book, so you can decide the best approach for your class. *Alternate reading* gives the class the chance to read a selection, individually or as a group, and then to have another individual or group read the next sentence or section. *Choral reading* permits students to read confidently and is a useful way to teach rhythm and intonation. *Echo reading* allows the students to imitate the teacher's intonation, pronunciation, and phrasing. Reading aloud should be done after the students have studied the text and can be done individually as well as with the group.

DURATION

It is best if you can allow up to three hours for each story, although a class at the advanced end of the beginner range might complete the work in one hour. It is rare for members of a beginner class to be of equal aptitude and skill, and the lower-level student needs more time than the more advanced. The non-core comprehension, vocabulary, and syntax/writing exercises will give the upper level of the class further opportunity to use English. The exercises in *Show What It Means* and *Are You Listening?* and the games and Total Physical Response activities should be done by the class as a group.

Only you, the teacher, know which exercises are suitable for your class on any given day, and I have tried to offer as much variety as possible at this level for you to choose from.

ACKNOWLEDGMENTS

I would like to thank David Barratt, Judi Hadfield, Margaret Hanson, Jim Turnbull, and Michael Vaughn-Rees, teachers at the Eurocentre, Lee Green, London, for their generosity with their time and expertise. I am very grateful for their help. My mistakes, of course, are my own.

Penny Cameron
Language & Culture Center
University of Houston
(On leave in London, 1993)

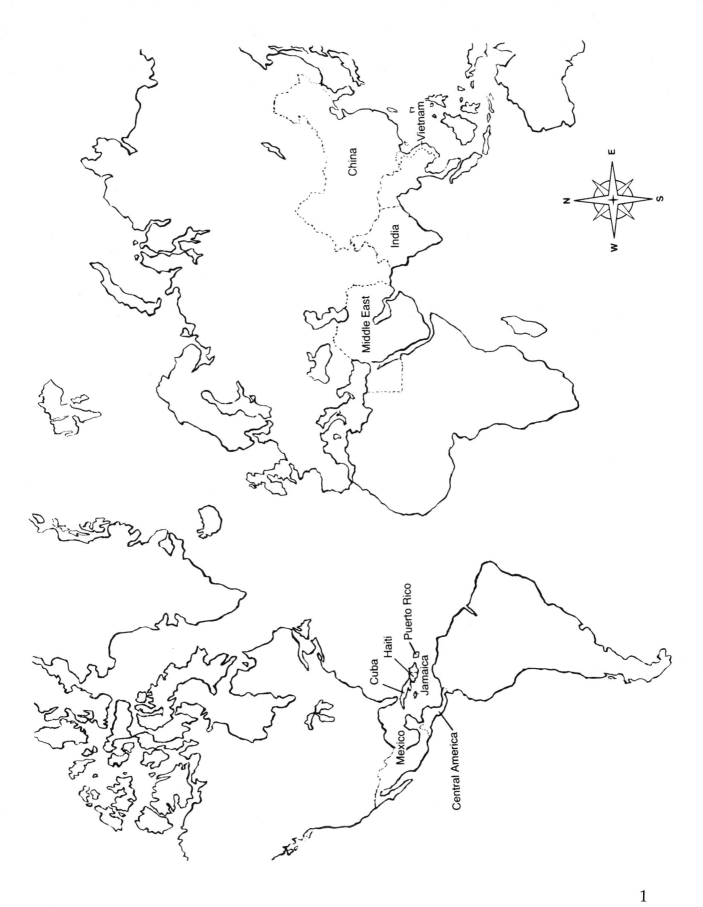

China

Vietnam

India

Middle East

N
E
W
S

Cuba

Haiti

Puerto Rico

Jamaica

Mexico

Central America

1

Look at the picture above. Talk about it with a partner.

1. Look at the map of North America. Point to Canada, the United States, and Mexico. Can you find the Great Lakes, the Mississippi, the Rio Grande, and the Rocky Mountains? Show them to your partner. Point to the places on the map you have visited.

2. Look at the map on page 1. Find the directions on the compass. Say the name of each one. What is north of this school? south? east? west?

3. What do you think happens in the story? Where are the people going? Are they walking or riding? Have you ever traveled a long way?

4. Why do you think the people are fighting?

5. Find the flag. What is in the picture on the flag? What kind of bird is it? What is it eating? What is the plant the bird is sitting on? Does this kind of bird live in your country?

Long, long ago the Aztec people went on a jouney to find a home. They traveled from the north. They went through the land that is now the United States. The trip lasted many years. Babies were born, grew
5   old, and died. The Aztecs kept walking. At last they came to Mexico.

The people were tired. "When can we stay in one place?" a man asked. "We want to stop and build our homes."

10   The priests said, "Our god Mexitla told us to go on. He told us there is a good place for us. The place is never too hot and never too cold. It's never too wet and never too dry. Mexitla will show us a sign when it's time to stop."

THE EAGLE AND THE SNAKE   3

"What will he show us?" the people asked. "How will we
know to stop?"

"We will see an eagle," the priest said. "A very large eagle,
like a king among birds."

"We see many large eagles," a woman said.

The priest said, "Our god Mexitla said that the eagle will
have a snake in its beak. The eagle will sit on a cactus plant and
eat the snake."

The people continued their long journey. They crossed rivers
and streams, and they climbed mountains. After a long time
they came to a lovely place that was not too hot and not too dry.

"This is a wonderful place," they said. "Maybe the eagle is
here." They waited for the eagle, but it did not come.

The priests said, "We cannot stay here. We will go on." So
the people traveled on.

"I want to find the eagle soon," a woman said. She sounded
very tired. Everyone agreed with her. They wanted to find the
eagle, too. They kept on walking. They hoped the land of the
eagle was not too far away.

At last the Aztecs came to a beautiful
place. It was a small strip of land next to a
pretty lake. The Toltec people who lived
there were angry. They tried to drive the
Aztecs away.

The Aztecs fought bravely. There were
many fierce battles. At last the Aztecs won.

One evening two priests walked around
the lake to look for a safe place to stay.

"There are many cactus
plants near this lake," one
priest said.

The other priest said, "Look! Up there!"

A large eagle flew overhead. Suddenly it dove
down and picked up a snake. As the priests
watched, it flew to the cactus. The eagle sat on
the cactus and ate the snake.

The Aztecs had their sign!
They built Mexico City at the
side of the beautiful lake.

Today you can see the eagle
and the snake on the flag of Mexico.

Are You Listening?

Turn to page 4. Find the words "This is a wonderful place" on line 25. Your teacher will read this part of the story. You read the book and listen. When you hear something different from the book, say "Excuse me" and tell your teacher what the book really says.

Example: Excuse me. The book says "wonderful," not "pretty."

What Did You Understand?

A. Underline the correct words. Follow the example.

(<u>Long ago</u>   yesterday   next year) the Aztec people were looking for a home. They (ran   rode   walked) from the (east   west   north). They were very (old   hot   tired), but they had to go on. They were waiting to see an eagle sitting on a cactus eating a (bird   snake   baby). At last they saw the sign, and built their city by the (river   sea   lake).

B. Talk to a partner. Choose the best summary of the story. A summary tells the most important part of the story in one or two sentences.

1. The Aztecs walked from Mexico toward the north. They went to New Mexico in the United States.

2. The Aztecs went through the land that is now the United States. At last they came to a beautiful place.

3. The Aztecs waited to see the eagle and the snake. Then they stopped and built their city. Today it is called Mexico City.

Show What It Means

Work with a partner. Answer the questions.

1. Who was tired in the story? Point to the line numbers where you find the answer.

2. Why were they tired?

Now show how you look when you feel tired.
Show how you walk and how you sit when you feel tired.

Work with Words

A. Work with a partner. Complete the sentences with the words in the box. Follow the example.

journey
eagle
bravely
safe
overhead
tired

1. An _e_ _a_ _g_ _l_ _e_ is a large bird.

2. _ _ _ _ _ people want to stop and rest.

3. Most babies feel _ _ _ _ when they are with their parents.

4. The Aztecs fought _ _ _ _ _ _ _ .

5. When something is above you, it is _ _ _ _ _ _ _ _ .

6. When you travel very far, it's a long _ _ _ _ _ _ _ .

B. Circle the word that is different. Follow the example.

1. hot   cold   wet   (city)

2. north   south   eagle   west

3. go   walk   travel   build

4. mountains   streams   rivers   lakes

5. beautiful   tired   lovely   pretty

6. Aztecs   at last   soon   never

Now compare answers with a partner. Did you choose the same words?

SEPARATETHEWORDS. SEPARATE/THE/WORDS.

Work with a partner. Put slashes between the words to separate them. Then dictate the sentences to your teacher, who will write them on the chalkboard.

TheAztecswalkedmanythousandsofmilestofinda placetobuildacity. Atlasttheysawthesign. An eaglesatonacactusandateasnake.

North, South, East, West

One student thinks of a country. The other students ask questions like "Is it north of here?" or "Is it south of Mexico?" The first student answers "yes" or "no" until someone correctly guesses the country's name. Then the student who guessed correctly thinks of a country.

How Do You Sound?

"I want to find the eagle soon," a woman said. She sounded very tired.

Take turns. Read these sentences to a partner. Then your partner will read them to you. Try to sound very dull and tired.

1. I have a lot of homework.

2. How far is it to the mall?

3. When does the bus come?

4. I don't want any dinner tonight.

5. I want to go home!

Now read the sentences again. This time, try to sound bright and energetic.

What Happened?

A. Write the correct answers. Follow the example.

1. Did the Aztecs walk for a long time or for a short time?

   *The Aztecs walked for a long time.*

2. Did the priests tell the Aztecs to look for an eagle eating a snake, or did they just tell them to keep walking?

   _____

3. Did the Toltecs welcome the Aztecs, or did they fight with them?

   _____

4. Did the Aztecs build a city by the lake, or did they look for another place?

   _____

B. Work with a partner. Here are some words from important parts of the story. Use them to make sentences to tell what happened in the story.

long journey	a sign	beautiful lake

Beyond the Story

Draw a flag you know well. Tell your classmates about your flag. Tell what colors are used in it and describe what it looks like.

Example:

This is the flag of the Olympic Games. It is white. There are five circles on it, one for each continent. The circles are blue, yellow, black, green, and red. The circles join together to show friendship.

Look at the pictures with a partner. Talk about them.

1. Find Haiti on the map on page 1.

2. Look at the picture. Find the man digging. His name is Bouki. What is piled on the ground?

3. What is the other man taking from Bouki? What do you think of this man? Do you trust him?

4. Find the three people near the middle of the picture. How do they feel? Here are some words to choose from: happy, sad, worried, angry, upset, surprised. When do you feel happy? angry? worried? surprised? sad? upset?

5. How does the man riding the horse in the last picture feel? What are the other people doing?

6. What happens when you *rent* a car? Circle the letter of the best answer:

   a. You pay money to the owner of the car. You use the car, and you keep it.

   b. You pay money to the owner of the car. You use the car, and then you give it back.

   c. You pay no money to the owner of the car. You use the car, and then you give it back.

7. What do you think happens in this story?

Bouki had a lot of yams in his garden. He dug them up and made a pile. It was time to take them to market.

Bouki looked at the big pile of yams. There were
5 too many for him to carry! "I want a horse or a donkey," Bouki said. He went to see his friend Moussa.

"Moussa," he asked, "can I borrow your donkey?"

10 Moussa looked sad and worried. "My donkey is not here," he said. "I can't find him anywhere. Ask Toussaint to lend you his horse."

"Ask Toussaint!" Bouki said. "That's a bad idea. Toussaint's so greedy! He wants money for everything."

15 "Can you sell the yams where they are?" Moussa asked.

"No," Bouki replied.

"Go to see Toussaint, then," Moussa said.

So Bouki went to Toussaint's house.
20 Toussaint showed Bouki his horse.

"He's a good horse," Toussaint said. "You can rent him for one day for fifteen dollars."

"Fifteen dollars! That's too much! I only
25 have five dollars," said poor Bouki.

"Give me the five dollars," Toussaint said. "You can get the horse tomorrow."

Bouki went home, feeling sad. The next morning, Moussa came to Bouki's house.

30 "My donkey is back!" Moussa called happily. "Now you can borrow him."

"I gave Toussaint five dollars," cried Bouki. "How can I get it back?"

Just then clever old Ti Malice came along. He listened to
35 Bouki's story, then he said, "I'm coming to see Toussaint with you. I think I can help."

Bouki and Ti Malice went to Toussaint's house.

"Where's the horse?" Ti Malice asked.

"Under the tree," Toussaint said. "Give me the ten dollars
40 Bouki owes me."

"How big is the horse?" asked Ti Malice. He took out a tape measure.

"He's a big horse," said Toussaint. "Now give me the money."

45 Ti Malice measured the horse's back. "Hmm," he said. "Bouki can sit in the middle. I can sit behind Bouki. Madame Malice can sit behind me. Madame Bouki can sit in front of Bouki."

50 Bouki smiled. He liked to sit with his wife.

"You can't put four people on a horse!" cried Toussaint.

"Bouki's children can go on the neck,"
55 Ti Malice continued.

"My poor horse!" Toussaint said. "He can't carry all those people!"

"He can try," said Ti Malice.

"You can't have him," Toussaint said. He was worried about
60 his horse.

Bouki kept smiling. He didn't understand that it was a bad idea to put so many people on one horse.

Ti Malice went on measuring the horse. "We can put my children between his ears," he said.

65 "You can't have him!" Toussaint yelled loudly.

"You took Bouki's money," Ti Malice said. "So he can have him." He turned to Bouki. "Where can we put the baby?"

"Baby?" Bouki said. "Baby?" He had no baby!

"Here are your five dollars back!" Toussaint said to Bouki.
70 "Now go away!"

"You rented him for fifteen dollars," Ti Malice said.

"Bouki gave me five dollars," Toussaint replied.

Bouki looked at the horse. "Where do we put grandmother?" he asked Ti Malice.

75 "Here!" Toussaint said angrily. "Take the fifteen dollars!" He gave Bouki ten more dollars. "Now give me my horse!" And he jumped on the horse's back and rode away.

Ti Malice laughed until he cried. Bouki didn't
80 understand why Ti Malice was laughing. At last Bouki said, "I'm glad he took his horse. There was no room for grandmother."

Are You Listening?

Turn to page 12. Find the words "Bouki had a lot of yams in his garden" on line 1. Your teacher will read this part of the story. You read the book and listen. When you hear something different from the book, say "Excuse me" and tell your teacher what the book really says.

Example: Excuse me. The book says "garden," not "house."

What Did You Understand?

A. Underline the correct words. Follow the example.

Bouki needed a horse or a donkey to carry his (baby   grandmother   yams) to market. Bouki went to see Moussa to (steal   buy   borrow) his donkey. Moussa's donkey was not there, so Bouki went to borrow Toussaint's horse. But Toussaint is very (greedy   kind   big). He wants (children   yams   money) for everything! Toussaint took five dollars from Bouki.

The next day, Ti Malice went to see Toussaint. He counted people to put on the horse. Toussaint was (happy   angry   poor). Ti Malice made Toussaint give Bouki (five   fifteen   fifty) dollars. Then Toussaint took his horse and rode away.

B. Number these events in the correct order. Follow the example.

_____ Ti Malice made Toussaint give Bouki fifteen dollars.

__1__ Bouki dug some yams.

_____ Bouki gave Toussaint five dollars to rent the horse.

_____ Moussa's donkey came back.

_____ Bouki went to see Toussaint.

Show What It Means

Work with a partner. Answer the questions.

1. Who was sad in the story? Point to the line numbers where you find the answer.

2. Who was worried in the story? Who was angry? Who was happy? Point to the line numbers.

Now show how you look when you feel happy.
Show how you look when you feel worried, angry, and sad.

Work with Words

A. Work with a partner. Complete the sentences with the words in the box. Follow the example.

yams
greedy
money
middle
yell
laugh

1. Bouki wanted to take his _y_ _a_ _m_ _s_ to market.

2. If you sit between two people, you are in the __ __ __ __ __ __ .

3. When you speak very loudly, you __ __ __ __ .

4. We use __ __ __ __ __ to pay for things.

5. When we think something is funny, we __ __ __ __ __ .

6. A person who wants money for everything is __ __ __ __ __ __ .

B. In this story Ti Malice talks about the people in a family. Work with a partner to fill in the chart. Follow the example.

WOMEN	MEN
Mother	_Father_
Daughter	_____
_____	Grandfather
_____	Uncle
Granddaughter	_____
Sister	_____
Niece	_____
Cousin	_____

SEPARATETHEWORDS. SEPARATE/THE/WORDS.

Work with a partner. Put slashes between the words to separate them. Then dictate the sentences to your teacher, who will write them on the chalkboard.

B o u k i w a n t e d t o b o r r o w a h o r s e t o c a r r y h i s y a m s t o t h e
m a r k e t . H e a s k e d T o u s s a i n t t o l e t h i m h a v e a h o r s e .
T o u s s a i n t w a n t e d m o n e y .

Act Like You Feel

Your teacher will tell you a feeling, and then an action. If the action goes with the feeling, do it. If the action does not go with the feeling, don't do it.

Example:
TEACHER: You are angry. Stamp your feet. [*Do it.*]
TEACHER: You are sad. Laugh. [*Don't do it.*]

How Do You Sound?

Turn to page 13. Listen as your teacher reads lines 75–78 .

Do you think Toussaint sounds angry? How can you tell?
How does your voice sound when you are angry?
Say "Give me my horse!" Try to sound very angry.

Take turns. Read these sentences to a partner. Then your partner will read them to you. Try to sound very angry.

1. I gave you five dollars.
2. I missed the bus.
3. Have you got my passport?
4. He took my key!

Connect the Sentences

Work with a partner. Connect the beginning of each sentence to the correct ending. Follow the example.

1. Toussaint was worried because
2. Moussa was sad because
3. Moussa was happy because
4. Toussaint was angry because
5. Ti Malice was laughing because

a. his donkey came back.
b. he paid fifteen dollars to Bouki.
c. Toussaint gave Bouki fifteen dollars.
d. his donkey ran away.
e. his horse was not big enough.

What Happened?

Write the correct answers. Follow the example.

1. Did Toussaint lend Bouki the horse, or did Bouki pay money for it?

   Bouki paid money for the horse.

2. Did Bouki borrow a donkey from Moussa, or did he rent a horse from Toussaint?

   _____

3. Did Toussaint take his horse away, or did he let Bouki use it?

   _____

4. Was Toussaint happy at the end of the story, or was he angry?

   _____

Describing People

Here are some words that describe different people in the story. Put a check mark under the name of the person they describe. Follow the example.

	BOUKI	TI MALICE	TOUSSAINT
clever		✔	
worried			
angry			
greedy			
silly			

Compare your list with two classmates. Ask your classmates how they chose the squares to mark. Now, with your partners, write a description of one person in the story. Follow the example.

Example: Bouki is silly. He doesn't understand about the horse.

Make It True

All these statements are false. Work with a partner. Write what is really true. Follow the example.

1. Bouki was a very clever man.

   Bouki was not a very clever man.

2. Toussaint wanted a lot of people to sit on the horse.

   _____

3. Toussaint kept Bouki's money.

_____

4. A big horse can carry ten people on its back.

_____

Beyond the Story

Here is a list of fruits and vegetables. Put them into two lists, one for fruits and one for vegetables. Put a check mark next to the ones that grow in your country. Follow the example.

banana yam melon tomato potato apple orange onion date pea
squash grape fig

FRUITS	VEGETABLES
banana	

Look at the picture above. Talk about it with a partner.

1. Find Jamaica on the map on page 1.
2. Look at the picture. Point to Tiger and Snake.
3. Who is Anansi? Do you think Anansi is strong? Do you think he is clever?
4. Why is the snake curled around the bamboo?
5. Point to the animals watching the snake. What do you think is happening?
6. Which is the longest line: A, B, or C?

    A.   _____

    B.   _____

    C.   _____

Tiger was the king of the jungle. When he roared, the other animals shook with fear. When Tiger spoke, the animals ran to obey him. Tiger was big and brave, proud and powerful.

Anansi the spider was little and timid, humble
5 and weak. The animals took no notice of him at all. When he spoke, nobody listened.

One night, when all the animals were together, Anansi said, "Tiger, you are the king of the jungle. All the animals do as you say. You own everything.
10 You know everything. Will you give me one little thing?"

Tiger flicked the end of his tail back and forth. "What do you want, Anansi?" he asked.

"I want the stories," Anansi said.

15 "The stories?" Tiger asked.

The other animals looked afraid. How dare Anansi ask for the stories? The stories were important! Whenever the animals came together, they told stories to each other. The stories helped them to understand the world. The stories told them who was
20 wise and who was foolish. The stories told them why things happened. The stories told them how to live their lives.

Tiger looked past Anansi as if he wasn't there. He growled a little. Then he said, "What do you want with the stories, Anansi?"

25 "I want you to call the stories Anansi stories," Anansi said.

The animals gasped in surprise.

Tiger decided to make a fool of Anansi and keep the stories for himself. He said, "Very well, Anansi, we will call the stories Anansi stories."

30 "Thank you, thank you," said Anansi.

"But first I have a little task for you," Tiger went on.

"Anything," said Anansi.

"You must catch Snake," Tiger said. "You must catch him and tie him up."

35 All the animals laughed out loud. That was impossible!

Anansi looked worried, but he said, "I will catch Snake for you, Tiger. And then the stories are mine!"

The other animals laughed. Silly Anansi! Clever Tiger!

Anansi went away and thought very hard. The next day he
40 tried to trap Snake, but Snake got away. The day after that, Anansi made another trap, but Snake escaped again. Then one night Anansi met Snake in the bamboo grove.

"Good evening, Snake," Anansi said. "I'm sorry you are not the longest thing in
45 the forest anymore."

"What do you mean?" Snake asked.

"Tiger says the bamboo is longer," Anansi said. "See? Here is a long piece of bamboo. I'm sure it's longer than you are."

50 Snake sniffed. "We'll soon see about that!" he said. He wound himself around the bamboo. Anansi ran up and down the bamboo.

"I can't see which is longer," Anansi
55 said. "I think you are moving up the bamboo."

"I'm not moving," Snake said.

"Maybe not," Anansi said, "but I can't say for sure that you are longer than the bamboo. Sorry." Anansi turned away.

"I know," said Snake. "Tie my tail to the bamboo. Then you know I can't move."

Anansi came back. "All right," he said. "Perhaps that will help." So he tied Snake's tail to the bamboo. Then he ran up to Snake's head.

"You're almost there!" Anansi said. "Stretch, Snake, stretch!"

Snake stretched. "I'm going around the bamboo," Snake said. "That makes me look shorter. Please tie my middle to the pole, Anansi. Then I can lie on the bamboo. I won't have to go around it."

Anansi did as he was asked, and tied Snake's middle to the pole.

The other animals came to watch. They saw Snake lying on the bamboo pole. He was nearly the same length.

"Stretch, Snake, stretch!" the animals called.

Snake stretched. His head didn't quite pass the top of the pole.

Anansi said, "If I tie your head to the pole, you'll be longer than the bamboo."

Snake said, "I am longer than the bamboo pole. I know it! Tie my head to the pole."

Anansi tied Snake's head to the pole. Tiger walked into the clearing. There was Snake, all tied up. The other animals watched Tiger.

Tiger smiled and said, "The stories are yours, Anansi." He did not want the other animals to see he was angry.

To this very day, people tell the Anansi stories and remember how clever little Anansi tricked Snake and won the stories from Tiger.

Are You Listening?

Look at page 22. Find the words "'Good evening, Snake,' Anansi said" on line 43. Your teacher will read this part of the story.
You read the book and listen. When you hear something different from the book, say "Excuse me" and tell your teacher what the book says.

Example: Excuse me. The book says "Snake," not "Tiger."

What Did You Understand?

A. Underline the correct words. Follow the example.

Anansi was (big   strong   <u>small</u>) and clever, and Tiger was big and strong. Anansi asked (Snake   Tiger   the other animals) for the stories. Tiger said that Anansi had a job to do: to (catch   eat   talk to) Snake. Everyone laughed. Anansi tried to trap Snake, but Snake (laughed   escaped   stretched). Then Anansi told Snake that he was not the longest thing in the (jungle   book   class). Snake let Anansi tie him to a piece of (bamboo   vine   rock). That is how Anansi won the stories.

B.   A summary tells the most important part of a story in one or two sentences. Talk to a partner. Choose the best summary of the story.

1.   Anansi wanted Tiger to give him the stories. Tiger told him to catch Snake. Anansi went to see Snake, and Snake said that he would help Anansi.

2.   Anansi asked Tiger for the stories. Tiger told Anansi to catch Snake. Anansi tricked Snake and tied him to a piece of bamboo. Tiger gave Anansi the stories.

3.   Anansi asked Tiger for the stories. Tiger told Anansi to catch Snake. Anansi caught Snake, but Tiger did not give him the stories. The other animals laughed at Tiger.

Show What It Means

Work with a partner. Show the action that goes with the underlined words.

Tiger <u>looked past</u> Anansi as if he wasn't there. (You look past your partner.)
He <u>growled</u> a little.
The animals <u>gasped</u> in surprise.
"<u>Stretch</u>, Snake, stretch!" (You stretch your arms if you can't stand up.)

Describe the Picture

Look at the picture on pages 20–21. Read the description. Work with a partner to cross out the words that do not describe the picture.

Example: Tiger is (~~biting~~/flicking) his tail.

Snake is very long. He is (sitting on the ground/twisted around a piece of bamboo). Anansi is (talking to/running away from) Tiger. Tiger's mouth is (open very wide/closed). He looks (a little surprised/very angry). The other animals are watching.

Work with Words

A. **Work with a partner. Complete the sentences with the words in the box. Follow the example.**

stories
bamboo
clever
trap
escaped
tie

1. _B a m b o o_ is a tall plant that grows in warm places.

2. The _ _ _ _ _ _ _ were important. They told the animals how to live.

3. When you _ _ _ a dog to a fence, it cannot run away.

4. You can catch a mouse in a _ _ _ _ .

5. Snake _ _ _ _ _ _ _ from Anansi's traps.

6. Anansi was very small, but he was _ _ _ _ _ _ .

B. **Fill in the chart with the differences between Tiger and Anansi.**

TIGER	ANANSI
big	_____
_____	timid
	humble
_____	
powerful	_____

Can you think of any other words that describe Anansi?

Work with a partner. Write them here:

_____

_____

Can you think of any other words that describe Tiger?

Work with a partner. Write them here:

_____

_____

Anansi Says

Your teacher is going to tell you things to do. If your teacher says "Anansi says," do the action. If your teacher does not say "Anansi says," don't do the action.

Example: TEACHER: Anansi says, stretch!   [*You stretch.*]

             TEACHER: Stand up!   [*You don't stand up.*]

How Do You Sound?

Listen to your teacher read this sentence.
Snake said, "I am longer than the bamboo pole. I know it!"

Snake sounds very sure!

Take turns. Read these sentences to a partner. Then your partner will read them to you. Try to sound very sure that you are right.

1. My friend was at <u>that</u> table.

2. I <u>did</u> pay for the groceries.

3. I came home at <u>five</u> o'clock.

4. I put my key on the <u>desk</u>.

5. <u>You</u> had the money.

What Happened?

Write the correct answers. Follow the example.

1. Did Anansi catch Snake the first time, or did he have to try again?

    Anansi had to try again.

2. Did Anansi trick Snake, or did Snake know that Anansi was trapping him?

    _____

3. Did Tiger keep the stories, or did he give them to Anansi?

    _____

4. Was Tiger happy at the end of the story, or was he angry?

    _____

Summarize the Story

Some of these statements are true and some are not. Rewrite them on a separate piece of paper and make all the statements true.   Then rewrite the true statements in the correct order to tell the story.

Tiger told Snake to catch Anansi.

Anansi was very clever and tricked Snake.

Anansi showed Snake a piece of bamboo.

Snake gave Anansi the stories.

Tiger asked Anansi for the stories.

My Favorite Part

What part of the story do people like best? Why? Ask your classmates.

Student's name   Favorite part   Reason

_____   _____   _____

_____   _____   _____

Beyond the Story

Do people in your culture have any stories about clever animals? Tell the stories to your classmates.

Look at the picture above. Talk about it with a partner.

1. Find the Middle East on the map on page 1.
2. Which man in the picture is rich? Which man is poor? How do you know?
3. The poor man is talking to a *mullah*, a very wise man. How does the poor man feel? Do you think the mullah will be able to help him?
4. Find the courtroom. Who is talking to the judge? Where have you seen that man before? What do you think will happen to the poor man?
5. Look at the man on the right side of the picture. What is he holding? What is he doing with it? What do you think happens in this story?

One day a poor man came into a little town. He was very hungry. Every time he saw food, his mouth watered. But he had no money.

The poor man stopped outside a fine restaurant.
5   The food at the restaurant smelled delicious. He sniffed and sniffed the wonderful smell.

The owner of the restaurant came into the street.

"Hey! You!" the owner called. "I saw what you did! You smelled my excellent food! I don't pay
10   cooks to make food for you to smell! You stole the smell of my food. Are you going to pay for it?"

The poor man replied, "I cannot pay. I have no money. I took nothing!"

The owner of the restaurant did not listen to him. "I'm
15 taking you to the judge," he said. And he took the poor man
to court.

The judge listened to the story. "This is very unusual," he
said. "I want to think about it. Come back tomorrow."

The poor man was very worried. He had no money. "What
20 can I do?" he asked himself. He could not sleep at all.

The next morning the man got up and
said his prayers. Then he went slowly
back to the court. On the way he met the
wise mullah, Nasrudin.
25 "Nasrudin," the poor man cried. "Please
help me. People say that you are very
clever. I am very unhappy and very
worried." He told Nasrudin his story.

"Well, well," wise Nasrudin said. "Let's
30 see what happens." The two
men went to court.

The judge was already there.
He was with the owner of the restaurant. They
looked very friendly with each other. When the
35 poor man arrived, the judge began to speak. He
said the poor man owed the restaurant owner a lot
of money.

Nasrudin stepped forward. "This man is my
friend," he said. "Can I pay for him?" He held out
40 a bag of money.

The judge looked at the restaurant owner. "Can
Nasrudin pay?" he asked.

"Yes," the restaurant owner said. "Nasrudin has money. The
poor man does not. Nasrudin can pay!"
45 Nasrudin smiled. He stood next to the restaurant owner.

Nasrudin held the bag of money near
the restaurant owner's ear. He shook it so
the coins made a noise.

"Can you hear the money?" he asked.
50 "Of course I can hear it," the restaurant
owner said.

"That is your payment," the mullah
said. "My friend smelled your food, and
you heard his money."
55 And that is the end of the story.

Are You Listening?

Look at page 30. Find the words "Nasrudin stepped forward" on line 38. Your teacher will read this part of the story. You read the book and listen. When you hear something different from the book, say "Excuse me" and tell your teacher what the book really says.

Example: Excuse me. The book says "forward," not "backward."

What Did You Understand?

A. Underline the correct words. Follow the example.

Once upon a time, a (poor   rich   tired) man stood outside a restaurant. He was (eating   taking   smelling) the food. The (mullah   owner   judge) came out of the restaurant and said the poor man was (buying   stealing   giving) the smell of his food. The owner took the poor man to court.

The poor man told Nasrudin what happened. Nasrudin was very (wise   poor   rich). Nasrudin went to court with the poor man, and promised to pay the fine. He let the restaurant owner (touch   listen to   take) his money. "That is your payment," the mullah said. "My friend smelled your food, and you heard his money."

B. Number these events in the correct order. Follow the example.

_____ The poor man asked Nasrudin to help him.

_____ The judge said to come back the next day.

_____ The restaurant owner said the poor man stole the smell.

_____ Nasrudin let the restaurant owner hear his money.

_____ The poor man met Nasrudin.

__1__ The poor man smelled the wonderful food.

Show What It Means

Work with a partner. Show what the words in the box mean.

1. sniff
2. step forward
3. shake (a bag)
4. go slowly (back to court)

Work with Words

Work with a partner. Complete the sentences with the words in the box. Follow the example.

wise	1. When you pay for something, you make a _p a y m e n t_ .
hungry	2. A _ _ _ _ _ _ _ _ _ _ is a place where you buy a meal.
owner	3. When food tastes good, it is _ _ _ _ _ _ _ _ _.
restaurant	4. Nasrudin was a very _ _ _ _ man.
delicious	5. When you have a house or car, you are the _ _ _ _ _.
payment	6. The poor man was very _ _ _ _ _ _, but he had no money to buy food.

How Do You Sound?

"Nasrudin," the poor man cried. "Please help me. People say that you are very clever. I am very unhappy and very worried."

Take turns. Read these sentences to a partner. Then your partner will read them to you. Try to sound very worried.

1. We have a test tomorrow.

2. Have you seen my keys?

3. I can't find my money.

4. How long will we be here?

Now read the sentences again. Try to sound very happy and not worried at all.

Tic Tac Toe

Divide into two teams, the X team and the O team. Play a game of tic tac toe on the chalkboard. The first team to get three Xs or Os in a row wins.

Now play tic tac toe with words. To win a square, a team member must say the word opposite in meaning to the word in the square he or she has chosen. If the other team says it is not the correct word, and your teacher agrees, they get a chance to say the correct word and win the square.

POOR	FAT	UP
SILLY	CANNOT	YES
RICH	FORWARD	HER

What Happened?

A. Write the correct answers. Follow the example.

1. Did the poor man eat in the restaurant, or was he still very hungry?

   The poor man was still very hungry.

2. Was Nasrudin a silly man, or was he a wise man?

   _____

3. Was the judge a friend of the restaurant owner, or was he a friend of the poor man?

   _____

4. Was the restaurant owner a kind man, or was he a cruel man?

   _____

5. Did Nasrudin pay the restaurant owner, or did he let him hear the money?

   _____

B. Both of these statements are false. Work with a partner. Write what really happened.

1. The restaurant owner said to the poor man: "Come in! Eat! The food is ready for you!"

   _____

2. Nasrudin gave the judge and the restaurant owner a lot of money.

   _____

EXPAND a Sentence

Work in groups of three and make these sentences bigger. Add one word at a time.

Here are some words you can use. You don't have to use all of them, and you can use words that are not on the list.

poor	clever	delicious	hungry	wise	smell
hungrily	wisely	very	food		

Example: *A man came into a town.*
           A poor man came into a town.
           A poor man came into a little town.

1. The man sniffed the food.

2. The teacher Nasrudin shook the bag.

Now compare your sentences with those of other groups.

Describing Things

A. What words do you think of when you think about food? Write as many words that describe food as you can:

_____   _____

_____   _____

_____   _____

_____   _____

What words did other people think of?

B. Write a description of a meal in your native country.

Example:

I ate at Toru's house last night with his family. We ate steamed rice and soup. Toru's mother cooked the food. I thought the food was delicious. After we ate we listened to Japanese music.

1. Where did you eat?

2. When did you eat?

3. Who was there?

4. What did you eat?

5. Who prepared the food?

6. How was the food?

7. What did you do after you ate?

I ate at _____ _____
                1   2

with _____ . We ate_____ .
           3   4

_____ cooked the food.   I thought the food
        5

was _____ . After we ate we _____
        6   7

_____ .

Beyond the Story

Bring in pictures of foods you like. Describe them to the class.

Look at the picture above. Talk about it with a partner.

1. Find Cuba on the map on page 1.
2. Point to the parts of the picture that show the day. Point to the parts of the picture that show the night.
3. What jobs do the men in the picture have? Which man is young? Which is older?
4. Write three words that describe the woman in the picture. Do you believe in ghosts? Why or why not?
5. Do you know these words?

   army   soldier   officer   sergeant   lieutenant

   Look at the picture. Point to the soldier, the sergeant, and the lieutenant.
6. What do you think happens in this story?

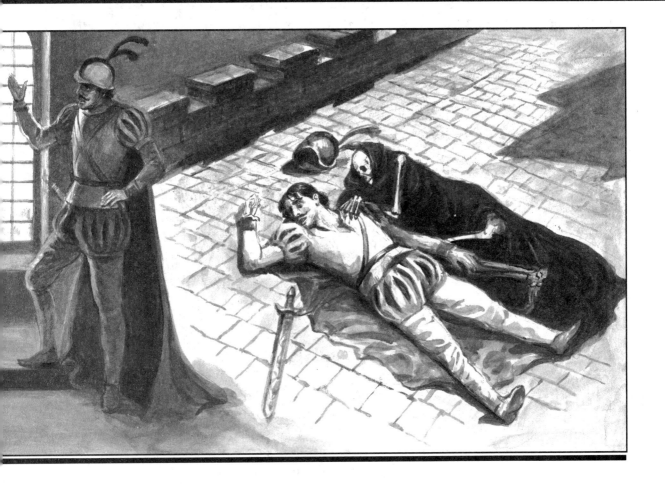

One morning a new young soldier was in Jagua Castle. It
was his first day in the army.

"Did the other soldiers tell you about the Blue Lady?" a
sergeant asked the new man.

5   "I don't think so," the young soldier
answered.

"They never tell new men about the Blue
Lady," the sergeant said. "They're afraid
that they'll run away." He looked at the
10 young soldier. "Don't go out on a moonlit
night," he said. "That's when she walks.
You don't believe me, do you? I tell you,
when the moon comes out, the Blue Lady
walks."

15   "What does she look like?" the young man asked the sergeant. "What does she do?"

    "Nobody goes close to her," the sergeant said softly. "All you see is a woman in blue. Her dress is long. She has a blue scarf over her head, so you
20 can't see her face. She walks outside the castle in the moonlight. She crosses the terrace, very slowly and quietly. She moves gracefully, the way a beautiful woman walks. I think she was a great lady."

    "What's her face like?" the young soldier asked.

25   "I told you, nobody knows," the sergeant replied. "Her scarf hides her face. Nobody will go close to her."

    "Have you ever seen her?" the young soldier asked.

    "Just once," the older man said. "She was walking in the moonlight. She went past me and walked straight up those
30 stairs. The moonlight showed her dark blue clothes. It was a warm night, but I felt cold when she passed me. Then she disappeared."

    "You mean you couldn't see her?"

    "She disappeared. She just vanished
35 while I was watching. One minute I saw her and then—nothing!" The sergeant spoke very softly now. It was hard to hear him. "But I know she was there," the sergeant went on. "The air felt different. I
40 felt sad. It was like someone I loved was dead."

    Just then the lieutenant came into the room. "Stop frightening the boy!" he said. "I forbid you to tell this ghost story!"

45   "But sir . . . " the sergeant began.

    "I will stop this silly story," the lieutenant said. "Tonight is the night of the full moon. I will watch the castle where she walks—or where you say she walks. I will go by myself. That will finish the story of the Blue Lady."

50   "Sir, I don't think . . . " the sergeant began.

    "Be quiet!" the lieutenant said. "Do your work. And stop frightening this boy!"

    The lieutenant left the room. "Nobody wants to watch where the Blue Lady walks," the sergeant said. "Nobody will
55 go alone."

    That night the lieutenant went to the terrace alone. It was a warm evening, and the moon shone brightly. The lieutenant was a brave man, but he prayed for the night to end.

The clock struck ten o'clock. "Only six more hours to go,"
60 the lieutenant said to himself.
       At eleven o'clock the moon seemed to get brighter. All the
soldiers were asleep. The lieutenant stood on the terrace, all
alone. The time passed slowly. It was nearly midnight, and the
night air was warm.
65   Then the lieutenant felt cold . . .

       The next morning the soldiers went to look for
the lieutenant. He lay on the terrace. He was alive.
Next to him lay a skeleton dressed in blue.
       "What happened?" the sergeant asked. The
70 lieutenant lay still, looking at the bones beside him.
       "What happened?" the soldiers asked again, but
the poor brave lieutenant said nothing.
       The soldiers carried the lieutenant to his bed.
Nobody saw him move, or heard him speak, ever again.

Are You Listening?

**Turn to page 39. Find the words "Did the other soldiers tell you about
the Blue Lady?" on line 3. Your teacher will read this part of the story.
You read the book and listen. When you hear something different
from the book, say "Excuse me" and tell your teacher what the book
really says.**

Example: Excuse me. The book says "soldier," not "man."

What Did You Understand?

A. Underline the correct words. Follow the example.

A soldier at Jagua Castle said that a (sergeant <u>ghost</u> officer) sometimes walked on the terrace. The ghost was a beautiful (woman man child) dressed in blue. She came at the full (sun stars moon). The (sergeant soldier lieutenant) went to watch for her alone. The next (afternoon morning night) the soldiers found him lying next to a (skeleton book door). He never spoke again.

B. Number these events in the correct order. Follow the example.

_____ The lieutenant was angry with the sergeant.

_____ The next day the soldiers found the lieutenant.

_1_ A new soldier came to Jagua Castle.

_____ The lieutenant went out to watch by himself.

_____ The lieutenant did not move or speak again.

_____ The sergeant told the new soldier a frightening story.

Show What It Means

A. Work with a partner. Answer the questions.

1. Who was frightened in the story? Point to the line numbers where you find the answer.

2. Why were they afraid?

3. You are driving very fast when another car drives straight in front of you. How do you feel? What do you do? What does your face look like?

B. Listen while your teacher reads lines 56–65. The reading begins: "That night the lieutenant went to the terrace alone."

Do you think the story sounds frightening?

What makes it frightening?

Read the end of the story to your partner or group. Try to sound very frightening.

Work with Words

Work with a partner. Complete the sentences with the words in the box. Follow the example.

cold
forbid
morning
night
old
alone

1. When you tell someone they cannot do something, you
   <u>f</u> <u>o</u> <u>r</u> <u>b</u> <u>i</u> <u>d</u> it.

2. It is dark during the __ __ __ __ __ .

3. The lieutenant went to watch by himself. He was __ __ __ __ __ .

4. When someone is young, they are not __ __ __ .

5. When the sun rises, it is the __ __ __ __ __ __ __ .

6. "Hot" is the opposite of "__ __ __ __ ."

Describe the Picture

Look at the picture on pages 38–39. Read the description. Work with a partner to cross out the words that do not describe the picture.

Example: It is morning/~~midnight~~.

The (lieutenant / new soldier) is lying on the castle terrace very close to a (tree / skeleton). He is (staring at / looking away from) the skeleton. The skeleton is wearing the same (blue gown /soldier's uniform) as the Blue Lady. We can see her skull. It's (night / morning).

Ghost Story

Take turns telling a ghost story. The first student begins by saying a simple sentence like "The ghost is a woman." The next student must repeat the sentence and add a word, or words. The next student must repeat both sentences and add another word or more words. The first student who forgets what the others have said is out.

Example: The ghost is a woman.
            The ghost is a woman. She walks at night.

Giving Orders and Making Requests

Listen as your teacher reads the following part of the story.

Just then the lieutenant came into the room. "Stop frightening the boy!" he said. "I forbid you to tell this ghost story!"

"But sir . . . " the sergeant began.

"Be quiet!" the lieutenant said. "Do your work. And stop frightening this boy!"

The lieutenant is giving orders. Listen again as your teacher reads the story. In the army, an officer gives orders to soldiers. But it isn't polite to give orders in everyday life. Instead, you can make polite requests.

Here are some polite requests. Practice saying them to your partner. Take turns.

1. Shut the door, please.
2. Pass me the book, please.
3. May I have a pencil?
4. Hand me that ruler, please.
5. Can you tell me the way to the bus?

Change these orders into polite requests. You may add words if you like. Work with your partner. Take turns.

1. Sit down!
2. Put it there.
3. Give it to me now.
4. Let go!
5. Tell me where the train station is.

What Happened?

Write the correct answers. Follow the example.

1. Was the lieutenant a brave man, or was he a coward?

   The lieutenant was a brave man.

2. Did the sergeant try to make the young soldier feel safe, or did he try to frighten him?

   _____

3. Was the sergeant laughing about the story, or did he believe it?

   _____

4. Do you think the Blue Lady really came, or do you think it is just a story?

   _____

What Do You Think?

Why do you think the lieutenant wanted to stop the story of the Blue Lady? Write your classmates' ideas below.

Student's name	Reason the lieutenant wanted to stop the story
_____	_____
_____	_____
_____	_____

Show What Happened

Mime the parts of the story where:

1. the sergeant is talking to the new soldier
2. the lieutenant sees the Blue Lady

Beyond the Story

Tell your classmates a ghost story from your country, but stop before the end. Your classmates have to guess how the story ends.

A. What do you know about monkeys? What do you know about crocodiles?

Work with a partner or group. Connect the beginning of each sentence to the correct ending. Follow the example.

1. Monkeys eat   a. the water.

2. Crocodiles eat   b. fruit and vegetables.

3. Monkeys live in   c. fish and small animals like monkeys.

4. Crocodiles live in   d. the trees.

5. Monkeys can   e. swim in the water and walk on land.

6. Crocodiles can   f. swing in the trees, but they can't swim.

Look at the picture above. Talk about it with a partner.

1. Find India on the map on page 1.
2. Where is your heart? Point to it.
3. Find the monkey swinging in the trees. Where is the crocodile?
4. Find the monkey on the crocodile's back. How does the monkey feel?
    Can he swim? What do you think the crocodile is going to do?
5. The crocodile takes the monkey back to land. Is the monkey safe now?
6. Find the crocodile sleeping next to the log. Why is he doing that?

Once, long ago in India, a monkey lived beside a river. He ate from the fig trees beside the water. He swung easily from tree to tree. He moved so lightly that he looked like a bird.

An old crocodile lived in the river under the fig
5   tree. He watched the monkey swing from tree to tree.

"If I had the monkey's heart," the crocodile thought, "I could be light and nimble too. I could move on land as easily as he does."

10   So every day the crocodile watched the monkey. He watched him swing from the trees. He watched him go to the river to drink. And all the time, he wanted the monkey's heart. As the crocodile watched, he thought of a plan . . .

One day the monkey came to the river to drink.

15   "Monkey," the crocodile said, "why do you eat figs? On the other side of the river there are bananas. They are large and sweet as honey."

The monkey loved to eat bananas.

"I know about those bananas," the monkey said sadly. "I
20   will never eat them, because they're on the other side of the river. And alas! There's no bridge. The water is deep and it moves quickly. I cannot swim, so I can never go to the other side."

The crocodile laughed. "Of course you can!" he said. "Get
25   on my back. I'll take you across the river."

The monkey jumped onto the crocodile's back, and the crocodile swam into the middle of the river. Then the crocodile said, "I'm going to kill you."

The monkey was very frightened. "Why are you going to kill
30   me?" he asked. "I'm only a thin monkey. I'm not fat enough to eat."

"I want your heart," the crocodile replied. "When I have your heart, I'll be able to swing in the trees, just like you do."

35   "Why didn't you tell me?" the monkey said. He pretended to laugh. "I don't have my heart with me. It's very dangerous for my heart when I swing from tree to tree. I take my heart out and hang it in the fig
40   tree. Look. Don't you see my heart hanging there among the red figs? Do you want me to get my heart?"

"Yes, yes," the crocodile said. "I see your heart,
45 hanging in the tree. I'll take you back to your side of
the river. We'll get your heart." And the crocodile
swam back to the monkey's side of the river.

The monkey ran away as soon as his foot
touched dry land. The crocodile watched the
50 monkey run away and said, "Ha! He tricked me
this time. Life is long! I'll think of something else."
Then he sank back into the brown water to make
his plans.

The crocodile watched the monkey every day. He watched to
55 see where the monkey went for water. The monkey always
went past a big piece of gray wood on his way to drink from the
river. This gray log was about the same color as the crocodile.
The crocodile crept out of the river and lay down beside the log.
He looked just like another piece of wood.

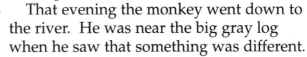

60   That evening the monkey went down to
the river. He was near the big gray log
when he saw that something was different.

"Good evening, gray log," the monkey
said.
65   The crocodile was quiet.

"Why are you quiet, gray log?" the
monkey asked. "You answer every other
night. Why are you quiet tonight?"

"Good evening, Monkey," said the
70 crocodile.

The monkey laughed. "Good evening,
Crocodile," he said. "I thought it was you. I'll keep my heart,
thank you!" And the monkey ran away and climbed a tree.

The crocodile never tried to catch the monkey again.   He
75 just lay in the water and wished he could swing in the trees. As
for the monkey, he looked down on the water and wished he
could swim across the river. He still wanted to eat the bananas
on the other side.

Are You Listening?

**Look at page 48. Find the words "'Monkey,' the crocodile said, 'why do
you eat figs?'" on line 16.   Your teacher will read this part of the story.
You read the book and listen. When you hear something different from
the book, say "Excuse me" and tell the teacher what the book really
says.**

Example: Excuse me. The book says "eat," not "buy."

What Did You Understand?

A. Underline the correct words. Follow the example.

There was once a crocodile who wanted to (eat   play   <u>swing</u>) in the trees. The crocodile watched the monkey and thought, "I want the monkey's (head   heart   hands)." The monkey did not know how to (run fly   swim). The crocodile took the monkey into the (trees   forest   river), and said he wanted his heart. The clever monkey tricked the crocodile. He said his heart was in the (water   bananas   fig tree). Then the crocodile pretended to be a (yellow   white   gray) log, but the monkey tricked him again.

B. Work with a partner. Some of these statements are true and some are false. Check True or False. If the statement is false, write what really happened. Follow the example.

	TRUE	FALSE
1. The crocodile wanted the monkey's foot.		✓

The crocodile wanted the monkey's heart.

2. The monkey told the crocodile that his heart was hanging in the fig tree.

_____

3. The monkey hid in the river and made his plans.

_____

4. The monkey pretended to be a big gray log.

_____

5. The monkey saw that the big gray log was really the crocodile.

_____

Show What It Means

Work with a partner. Answer the questions.

Who moved lightly in the story, the monkey or the crocodile? Point to the line number where you find the answer.

Pick up something from a table. Pretend it is heavy. Now pick up the same thing and pretend it is light.

Show how you move when you are carrying something heavy.

Show how you move when you are carrying something light.

Work with Words

A. Work with a partner. Complete the sentences with the words in the box. Follow the example.

monkey
banana
swing
swim
heart
log

1. A _l_ _o_ _g_ is a large piece of wood.

2. A __ __ __ __ __ __ lives in the trees.

3. Your __ __ __ __ __ pumps blood around your body.

4. Are you safe in the water? Can you __ __ __ __ ?

5. A __ __ __ __ __ __ is a fruit with a yellow skin.

6. Animals that live in trees can often __ __ __ __ __ from branch to branch.

B. Circle the word that is different. Follow the example.

1.	monkey	rabbit	crocodile	(tree)
2.	fig	fish	apple	banana
3.	river	water	sea	bridge
4.	dry	gray	brown	red
5.	hand	land	foot	heart
6.	run	reply	swim	swing

Now compare answers with a partner. Did you choose the same words?

Animal Twenty Questions

One student thinks of an animal. The other students ask yes/no questions until someone guesses the animal. The person who guesses correctly thinks of another animal.

Example: Does the animal swing from tree to tree?

How Do You Sound?

"Monkey," the crocodile said, "why do you eat figs? On the other side of the river there are bananas. They are large and sweet as honey."

The crocodile is trying to make the bananas sound very good!

Take turns. Read these sentences to a partner. Then your partner will read them to you. Try to make the thing you are talking about sound so good that everyone will want it.

1. This car has gone 10,000 miles.
2. The fruit is very ripe.
3. This chicken is so spicy!
4. This is a very soft bed.
5. What an interesting idea!

Now read the sentences again. Make the things sound very undesirable, so nobody will want them.

What Happened?

Write the correct answers. Follow the example.

1. Did the story happen in India or in France?

    The story happened in India.

2. Was the monkey clever, or was he silly?

    _____

3. Do monkeys swim very well, or are they good at swinging through the trees?

_____

4. Did the crocodile want the monkey's heart, or did the monkey want the crocodile's heart?

_____

Ask the Class

Go around the class and ask people if they want to be a monkey or a crocodile. Then ask them for their reasons.

Student's Name	Monkey	Crocodile	Reason

Beyond the Story

Prepare notes about an animal from your country. Here are some things to think about:

What is the animal's name?
How big is it?
What does it look like?
Does it have fur?
What does it eat?
Is it dangerous?
Where does it live?
Does it come out in the day or at night?

Be ready to talk to the class or your group.

Look at the picture above. Talk about it with a partner.

1. Find Guatemala and other countries in Central America on the map on page 1.

2. Find the Moon God walking across the sky. Is it day or night? Is the Moon God happy or angry?

3. What is the Moon God doing with the turtle? Why do you think this is happening?

4. Find the place where the Moon God is in two places at the same time. What are the two places? Does it look like he got smaller?

5. What is finally happening to the moon? Have you noticed this happening to the moon?

Once upon a time the moon was always big and
round and full. In those days the Moon God lived
in a cave. At night he left his cave and climbed into
the sky. He walked across the sky all night.

5   When the morning came, the Moon God returned
home to his cave. His home was very beautiful.
The cave was made of coral, and it was shaped like
a snail shell. There was just enough room for him.

One morning the Moon God went home as usual.
10 He was tired, and very ready to go to bed and sleep,
but something was wrong. There was a small green
turtle lying on his bed!

"What are you doing here?" the Moon God asked. "This is a
very small bed. There isn't enough room for both of us."

15 The Moon God was very tired, so he threw the little turtle out of the cave.   Soon he was asleep.

The next night the Moon God got up and walked across the sky as usual. When he came home he looked at his bed. There was a medium-sized turtle lying in it.

20 "Get out!" the Moon God yelled. "I want to go to sleep." He threw the turtle out of the cave. It was more difficult to move this turtle, because it was bigger.

The next morning the Moon God hurried home.
25 He wanted to see if there was another turtle in his bed.

This time, the turtle was very big. It took the Moon God a long time to drag it out of the bed. He was very angry, and it was hard for him to sleep.

30 "I can't live like this," he said to himself. He went to see his friend the Water God.

"I'm so tired I can hardly walk!" he complained. "How can I light the sky when I'm tired? I need my sleep."

The Water God had an idea. "I can stay in your cave while
35 you are out," he said. "I will guard your cave and stop turtles from getting in. If I want to make it rain, you can come home."

The Moon God thanked him and went out to walk across the sky.

The Water God guarded the Moon God's cave for a few
40 nights. The Moon God slept peacefully. But one night the Water God did not come, so the Moon God stayed home to guard his cave. The sky was dark all night.

The Moon God was not sure what to do if the Water God did not come again. He thought and thought. Then he had an idea.
45 "I can leave part of myself in the cave," he said.

That night, only a small part of the Moon God went to walk across the sky. The night was dark, but the Moon God was

happy. He knew there were no
50 turtles in his cave. The next night the Moon God was a little bigger in the sky. There was a little less of him in the cave.

Every night the Moon God took more of himself to the sky. When he was not
55 worried about turtles, the moon was full. But when he started to think about green turtles again, the moon got smaller. And so it goes, from that day to this. That is why the moon changes its size
60 and shape.

Are You Listening?

Turn to page 55. Find the words "One morning the Moon God went home as usual" on line 9. Your teacher will read this part of the story. You read the book and listen. When you hear something different from the book, say "Excuse me" and tell the teacher what the book really says.

Example: Excuse me. The book says "home," not "back."

What Did You Understand?

A. Underline the correct words. Follow the example.

There was a small (red   blue   green) turtle in the Moon God's bed when he came home one (night   day   morning). He threw it out and went to sleep. The next morning the Moon God found (a fish another turtle   the Water God) in his bed. This one was bigger and more difficult to throw out. Then the Moon God found a very big turtle.

He went to see his friend the Water God. The Water God agreed to (guard   close   empty) the cave while the Moon God was out. But one night the Water God did not come to the cave. The next night the Moon God divided (the Water God   himself   the turtle) in two parts. He left part of himself in the (sea   sky   water) and part in the cave.

That is why the moon changes its size and shape.

B. Work with a partner. Some of these statements are true and some are false. Check True or False. If the statement is false, write what really happened. Follow the example.

	TRUE	FALSE
1. The Moon God lived in a cave.	✓	
2. The Moon God decided never to leave his cave.		
3. The Moon God sometimes sends part of himself into the sky.		
4. We can see the moon getting bigger and smaller every month.		

Show What It Means

Work with a partner. Answer the questions.

1. Who was tired in the story? Why? Point to the line number where you find the answer.
2. How do you look when you feel tired? Show how tired people sit.

Work with Words

A. Work with a partner. Complete the sentences with the words in the box. Follow the example.

cave
bed
medium
turtle
threw
rain

1. The Moon God found a _t_ _u_ _r_ _t_ _l_ _e_ in his bed.

2. When something is not very big or very small it is __ __ __ __ __ __ -sized.

3. A __ __ __ __ is a hollow place underground or in the side of a hill.

4. When you have an umbrella, you don't worry about the __ __ __ __ .

5. When you're tired, you want to go to __ __ __ .

6. I did not want to keep my old clothes, so I __ __ __ __ __ them away.

B. Draw pictures of the full moon, a half moon, a quarter moon, and a crescent moon.

What color is the moon? Is it always the same color?

Work with a partner and write a sentence about the moon.

How Do You Sound?

Turn to page 56. Listen as your teacher reads lines 30–33.

Do you think the Moon God sounds tired? How can you tell?

Take turns. Read these sentences to a partner. Then your partner will read them to you. Try to sound very tired.

1. It's nine o'clock.
2. Are you ready to go?
3. We leave in twenty minutes.
4. It's ten miles away.

Now read the sentences again. This time, try to sound very awake and alert.

Trip to the Moon

You are going to the moon! What will you take with you? The first student thinks of something beginning with A, the second student thinks of something beginning with B, and so on.

What Happened?

Write the correct answers. Follow the example.

1. Was the Moon God happy to see the turtles, or was he angry?

   The Moon God was angry to see the turtles.

2. Did the Water God help the Moon God, or did he say he was too busy?

   _____

3. Did the Moon God go to the Water God's house to live, or did he stay in his own cave?

   _____

4. Did the Moon God let the turtles have his bed, or did he keep them away?

   _____

5. Did the Moon God leave the sky forever, or did he find a way to be in two places at the same time?

   _____

Find the Story

There are two stories in the paragraph below. One is about the Moon God and the other is about Anansi and the stories. Underline the sentences that tell the story of the Moon God. Follow the example.

Anansi was very clever. He wanted to own the stories. The Moon God was very angry about green turtles. Tiger said, "You catch Snake, Anansi. Then I'll give you the stories." He found them in his bed. At first it was not so bad, because the turtle was little and easy to throw out of the cave. All the animals laughed at Anansi. The next time, however, the turtle was larger. But Anansi caught Snake, and Tiger gave him the

stories.   The Moon God decided never to let a turtle into his cave again.

Now he leaves part of himself in the cave to keep the turtles away.

How did you know which sentences to choose?

Now rewrite the two stories on a separate sheet of paper.

Beyond the Story

**In the United States, people say they see a man in the moon. Talk to
your classmates and find out what people in their native countries see
in the moon. Complete the chart. Sometimes people from the same
country will see different things.**

STUDENT'S NAME	NATIVE COUNTRY	WHAT PEOPLE SEE IN THE MOON

Look at the picture above. Talk about it with a partner.

1. Find Puerto Rico on the map on page 1.
2. Point to the man holding the bird. His name is Pedro Animala. Say three words to describe him. Where do you think he got the bird?
3. Find the woman. What is she doing? What do you think Pedro Animala will do next?
4. Who is Pedro listening to? What do you think he hears?
5. Look at the right side of the picture. Is the woman happy or unhappy? Who is the man?

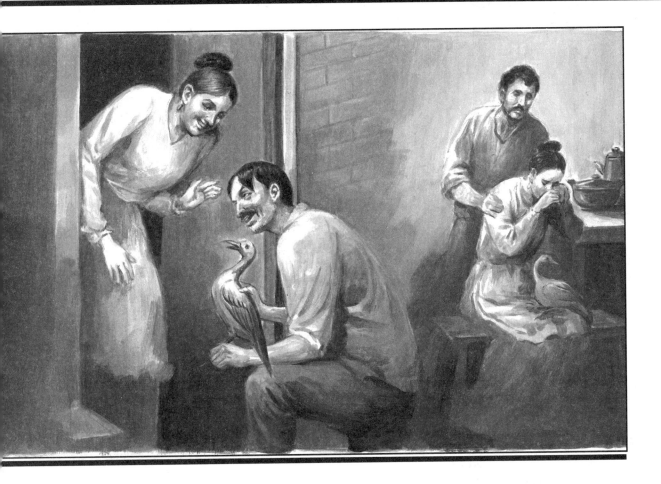

There once was a trickster called Pedro Animala.
He lived long ago in the mountains of Puerto
Rico. He did not have a rich family, and he never
worked at a job. How did he earn money? He lived
5 by tricking people.

One day Pedro trapped a young carrao bird.
"What good luck," he thought. "Now I can sell it."
So off to town he went, whistling happily as he
walked.

10 On his way to town Pedro passed a neat, little
house. He could see a woman inside the house. She
was carefully putting papaya candy on a plate. He walked closer to the window and heard her say, "How happy my
husband will be! I'll hide this candy and we'll eat it after dinner
15 tonight! I'll hide it quickly, before he comes home." Pedro

looked through the window and saw the woman put the plate at the very back of the cupboard.

Pedro hurried back to the road. He had
20 an idea . . .

Pedro held the carrao bird firmly under his arm and marched up to the woman's front door.

"Good afternoon," he said politely.
25   "Good afternoon," the woman replied.
Pedro thought she might go inside, so he said quickly, "Would you like to buy this bird?"

"Why would I buy it?" the woman asked. "I don't really need a carrao bird. Can I eat its eggs? Does it sing like a
30 canary? What can a carrao bird do?"

"This is a special bird," Pedro said solemnly. "It can tell you what happened in the past and what will happen in the future."

The woman did not believe him. "Show me," she said.

"Are you sure you want to know?" Pedro asked.
35   The woman was curious now. "Yes, of course," she said. "Show me what your bird can do."

Pedro tapped the bird on its head. "Carrao, carrao!" it said. Pedro leaned down to listen to it. He smiled and said, "The bird says that you put
40 some papaya candy into your cupboard."

The woman was amazed, but she tried to hide her feelings. "Show me some more," she said.

Pedro tapped the bird on the head again. It cried out, "Carrao, carrao!" Pedro put his head near the
45 bird's beak. He listened to it very carefully. "The bird says that your husband will be home soon for his dinner," Pedro said.

"This is an amazing bird," the woman said. "How much do you want for it?"
50   "Fifty pesetas," Pedro said.

The woman gave Pedro Animala the money, and he went away as quickly as his feet could carry him.

The woman carried the bird into the house and sat down with it. She tapped it on the head.
55   "Carrao, carrao," the bird said. The woman put her head close to the bird's beak. She could not understand anything. She tapped the bird on the head again. She was so busy listening to the bird, she did not hear her husband come in.

"What are you doing?" her husband asked.

60   "I'm waiting to hear what the bird says," she answered. "This bird can tell the future."

    "It's just a carrao bird," her husband said. "All it can say is its name, 'carrao! carrao!' Where did you get it from?"

    "I bought it from a man who came to the door," the wife
65 replied.

    "And I just saw Pedro Animala and he looked very happy," her husband said.

    The woman felt sick. Her face turned red, then white, and then red again. "Do you mean I bought
70 this bird from Pedro Animala?" she asked. "I feel so silly!" She began to weep.

    "Don't cry, my dear," her husband said. "Pedro Animala tricks everybody."

    The poor woman still waits for Pedro to return so
75 she can get her money back. But she will never see him again, because Pedro Animala never goes to the same place twice.

Are You Listening?

Turn to page 63. Find the words "There once was a trickster called Pedro Animala" on line 1. Your teacher will read this part of the story. You read the book and listen. When you hear something different from the book, say "Excuse me" and tell the teacher what the book really says.

Example: Excuse me. The book says "mountains," not "hills."

What Did You Understand?

A. Underline the correct words. Follow the example.

    There once was a (good man <u>trickster</u> student) called Pedro Animala. Pedro went to a woman's (school   office   home). "I have a (bird   animal   man) that can tell the future," he said. The poor woman believed him and (stole   bought   fed) the bird. (The next week The next day   Soon) she saw that the bird was just an ordinary bird. She felt very (silly   happy   pleased).

B. Work with a partner. Some of these statements are true and some are false. If the statement is false, write what really happened. Follow the example.

	TRUE	FALSE

1. Pedro Animala stole a carrao bird.

   Pedro Animala trapped a carrao bird.   ✓ (FALSE)

2. Pedro understood what the bird was saying.

   _____

3. The woman in the story believed everything that Pedro told her.

   _____

4. Pedro Animala tricked the woman's husband.

   _____

Show What It Means

Work with a partner. Answer the question.

Who feels sick in the story? Point to the line number where you find the answer.

Show how you look when you feel sick or when something has gone wrong. Show how you move and how you sit.

Work with Words

Work with a partner. Complete the sentences with the words in the box. Follow the example.

trickster	march	canary	future	curious
busy	silly			

1. When you feel foolish, you feel _s i l l y_.

2. A _ _ _ _ _ _ is a bird that sings beautifully.

3. When you want to know more, you are __ __ __ __ __ __ __.

4. People who are __ __ __ __ have a lot to do.

5. Someone who tricks people is a __ __ __ __ __ __ __ __ __.

6. Yesterday is in the past, tomorrow is in the __ __ __ __ __ __.

7. When you walk like a soldier you __ __ __ __ __.

Change the Story

Look at the pictures on pages 62–63, and change the story. Each student says a sentence and changes a detail so it is false. The other students correct the sentence.

Example: Pedro Animala was a hardworking man.
No, Pedro Animala was a trickster.

What Happened?

A. Write the correct answers. Follow the example.

1. Was Pedro Animala a trickster or an honest man?

Pedro Animala was a trickster.

2. Did Pedro really understand what the bird was saying, or did he pretend to understand?

_____

3. Did the woman in the story believe everything Pedro told her, or did she know he was tricking her?

_____

4. Did Pedro Animala trick a lot of people, or did he trick only that one woman?

_____

5. Could the carrao bird really tell the future, or could it only say its name?

_____

B. Work with a partner. Answer the questions. Look back at the story if you need help.

1. "Pedro . . . marched up to the woman's front door." (lines 21–23)
Why do you think the author said "marched"? Why not just "walked"?

2. "The woman was amazed, but she tried to hide her feelings."(lines 41–42)
Why do you think the woman wanted to hide her feelings?

3. "The woman gave Pedro Animala the money, and he went away as quickly as his feet could carry him." (lines 51–52)
Why was he in such a hurry?

4. "But she will never see him again, because Pedro Animala never goes to the same place twice." (lines 75–77)
Why doesn't Pedro go to the same place twice?

Scrambled Sentences

The words in these sentences are out of order. Rewrite the sentences on a separate sheet of paper so they agree with the story.

1. sell to Pedro a bird wanted.

2. the tricked Pedro woman.

3. very was happy Pedro.

4. head the bird The tapped the woman on.

5. husband the wife home came and his The bird listening found to.

Ask the Class

Interview your classmates and ask their opinions about Pedro. Do they think Pedro will ever be a hardworking person? Why or why not? How do they think Pedro should be punished for tricking people?

STUDENT'S NAME	OPINION: WILL PEDRO EVER BE A HARDWORKING PERSON?	REASON	PUNISHMENT

Beyond the Story

"This is an amazing bird," the woman said. "How much do you want for it?"

"Fifty pesetas," Pedro said.

The woman gave Pedro Animala the money, and he went away as quickly as his feet could carry him.

In the story the woman does not bargain with Pedro. She just pays the price he asks. When you bargain, you argue. The seller says he wants ten dollars for something. The buyer says she'll pay five. The seller says nine dollars, and so on.

Work with a partner. One of you has something to sell. The other person wants to buy it. Bargain to decide what the price will be. Practice and then do your bargaining in front of the class.

Look at the picture above. Talk about it with a partner.

1. Find Vietnam on the map on page 1.

2. Find the princess in the palace. Describe her. What is she looking at?

3. Point to the boatman bowing to the princess. How does the princess feel? Why do you think she looks so surprised and upset?

4. Find the boatman's family. What have they found?

5. Point to the princess looking into the goblet. What does she see? What do you see? Is there magic in this story?

6. What do you think happens in this story?

Once upon a time there was a princess. She had
no friends and was very lonely. She lived with her
father in a palace full of wonderful things, but she
was not happy. She often looked out her window to
5 see the river far below the palace. She felt sad and
alone.

The princess watched the river at the same time
every day. She waited for a fishing boat that came
every afternoon. Every day she watched the
10 boatman. She heard him sing. And oh! How sad
and beautiful his songs were!

Each day the princess hurried to her window to hear the
boatman. "His voice is so clear," she thought. "I wonder what
he looks like. Is he handsome? Is he strong?" But the boatman

15 was too far away for the princess to see.

For months she listened to his beautiful sad song. She
dreamed her dreams, and she told nobody about the boatman.
Then one afternoon, the boatman did not come. The princess
waited quietly.

20 The next day he did not come. The day after that she
watched the river. No little boat floated beneath her window.

The princess went to bed. She was too sick to get up, too sick
to move. Her father, the king, called the best doctors. They
could find nothing wrong with the princess. She lay in her bed,
25 pale and tired.

Then, one day, she heard a wonderful sound. A song came
up from the river. The princess went to the window. It was her
boatman. His beautiful voice made her feel better at once. Her
father, the king, was very happy.

30 The king said to his servants, "Who is this man? His song
has made my daughter well again. Go and bring him to me."

The people at the palace went out to find the boatman. They
brought him back to the king.

The king sent a servant to find his daughter. "Your father
35 found the boatman with the sweet voice," the servant said.
"His name is Truong-Chi. He's with your father now. Your
father says the boatman is a fine man."

Quickly the princess put on her finest clothes. Then she ran
downstairs. The boatman was talking to her father. His back
40 looked strong. The princess heard her heart beating loudly.
Could the boatman hear it too?

The boatman turned around and
bowed. The princess held her breath. Was
he handsome? Then she saw his face, and
45 she was so shocked she felt sick. This was
not the man of her dreams! This man's
face was ordinary and ugly. The princess
looked away. She was a young girl and
saw only what people looked like. She had
50 no idea if people were good or bad, kind or
cruel.

"Come, my dear," the king said, but the
princess turned and ran from the room.

The king sent the boatman away. But the poor boatman's life
55 had changed forever. He loved the princess and knew his love
was hopeless. She did not love him. The poor boatman did not
eat or drink. He was far from his home, and nobody was there
to help him. He did not sing any more. At last his poor heart
broke, and he died of grief and sadness.

60 　　Years later, his family came to take his body out of its grave. They wanted to rebury him with the rest of his family. When they opened the grave, they did not find a body. In its place there was a beautiful piece of crystal. The wonderful crystal
65 was clear, like fine glass. It sparkled whenever the light fell on it.

　　The family put the crystal on the front of their boat. One day the king saw it, and bought it from them.

70 　　The king took the crystal to a clever workman and said "Make this crystal into a goblet."

　　The goblet was beautiful! People came from miles around just to see it. One day the king put some tea into the goblet and
75 something wonderful happened. Truong-Chi appeared, rowing his boat in the tea.

　　The king called the princess. She still lived in the palace, and she was still lonely and unhappy. When she saw the tiny
80 Truong-Chi, she wept. One of her tears fell into the tea, and the goblet disappeared. Nobody ever saw the goblet, or Truong-Chi, again.

Are You Listening?

Look at page 72. Find the words "The king said to his servants . . ." on line 30.

Your teacher will read this part of the story. You read the book and listen. When you hear something different from the book, say "Excuse me" and tell your teacher what the book really says.

Example: Excuse me. The book says "man," not "fellow."

What Did You Understand?

Underline the correct words. Follow the example.

There was a lonely princess in (Holland Mexico <u>Vietnam</u>). She looked out her window and saw a man named Truong-Chi rowing a little boat. He sang beautifully and she (hated fell in love with disliked) his voice. Then he went away.

The princess became very (happy sick angry). She lay in her bed, and nobody was able to help her. Then she heard the boatman's (song name face) again. She recovered immediately.

The king brought the boatman to the (palace house river). When the princess saw his face, she (ran away was sick again ran to kiss him). The boatman died of grief. His body became a beautiful piece of crystal. The king bought the crystal and a craftsman made it into a beautiful (bowl mug goblet). One day a wonderful thing happened. The king and the princess saw Truong-Chi rowing his boat in the goblet! The princess wept, and Truong-Chi (came back disappeared sang) forever.

B. Number these events in the correct order. Follow the example.

_____ The princess saw that the boatman was ugly and she ran away.

_____ The boatman came back and the princess heard his song.

__1__ The princess fell in love with the boatman's voice.

_____ The king brought the boatman to the palace.

_____ The poor boatman died of a broken heart.

_____ The boatman went away and the princess became very sick.

Work with Words

A. **Work with a partner. Complete the sentences with the words in the box. Follow the example.**

alone
crystal
handsome
window
servant
pale

1. A _s e r v a n t_ is someone who is paid to work in another person's house.

2. When you are __ __ __ __ your face has lost its color.

3. To see outside, look out the __ __ __ __ __ __ .

4. When you do something by yourself, you do it __ __ __ __ __ .

5. __ __ __ __ __ __ __ is very clear glass.

6. When a man is good-looking, we say he is __ __ __ __ __ __ __ __ .

B. **Which of these words and phrases describe the boatman and the princess? Work with your partner, and put them in the correct column. You don't have to use every word, and you may add words. Follow the example.**

beautiful	kind	silly	strong	lonely
truthful	cruel	unkind	sang beautifully	
ugly	sad	waited patiently		

PRINCESS	BOATMAN
beautiful	

Be ready to say why you put the words where you did.

That's in the Story

One student thinks of a person or thing in the story. The other students ask yes/no questions until one of them guesses who or what it is. Then that student thinks of someone or something in the story.

Example: Is it a person?
             Yes.

How Do You Sound?

How do people sound when they are sad? Listen as your teacher reads the end of the story to you. Why does it sound sad?

Take turns. Read these sentences to a partner. Then your partner will read them to you. Try to sound very sad.

1. There's no more bread left.

2. Do you have any food?

3. I have some money left.

4. I have ten dollars.

5. I saw John in the classroom.

6. I want Mary to come here.

7. I want to call my mother.

8. I like chicken for dinner.

Now say the same sentences in a very happy voice.

What Happened?

Write the correct answers. Follow the example.

1. Was the princess clever and wise, or was she a silly, young girl?

    The princess was a silly, young girl.

2. Did the king like the boatman, or did he dislike him?

    _____

3. Did the boatman love the princess, or did he forget her quickly?

    _____

4. Was the crystal goblet beautifully made, or was it rough and ugly?

    _____

5. Was the princess happy at the end of the story?

    _____

6. Does this story make you feel sad or happy?

    _____

Beyond the Story

In English there is an expression: "Beauty is in the eye of the beholder."   (The beholder is the person who is looking at something.) Talk to a partner. What do you think it means? Is there a saying like it in your first language? What is it? What does it mean in English? Share your saying with your classmates.

Look at the picture above. Talk about it with a partner.

1. Find China on the map on page 1.
2. How many women are swimming in the pond? Do you think they are part of the same family? What is the man doing?
3. Find the grandmother. How does she feel?
4. Do you know about the Milky Way? It's the bright part in the sky with a lot of stars. In China, it is called *the silver stream of heaven.* Find the Milky Way in the picture. What else do you see?
5. Point to the birds. What are they doing? What do you think the man and woman will do now?

Once upon a time the seven granddaughters of
the Queen of Heaven were swimming in a pond on
earth. The pond was in a very quiet place, and they
did not think anyone was nearby. They played in
5 the water, and laughed, and splashed each other.
Their clothes lay in neat piles beside the pond.

The seven sisters did not know that a cowherd
was watching them. The cowherd quickly took one
of the piles of clothes and ran to his hut. "I hope
10 these belong to the sister with the very long hair,"
he thought. "She is so beautiful." He waited quietly to meet the
young woman who owned the clothes.

After a while the sisters grew tired of the pond. They came
out of the water and got dressed. But one sister, the youngest,

15 could not find her clothes. And without her magic clothes, she could not fly back to heaven.

All the sisters searched everywhere, but it was no use. They lent the youngest sister enough clothes to cover her. Then the six sisters kissed the youngest goodbye and flew back to heaven.
20 Their youngest sister was left alone, weeping bitterly. She was cold, and she needed to find shelter. She went a little way from the pond and saw a small hut. She knocked gently on the door.

The cowherd opened the door. He saw the girl with long hair standing there. Quickly, he gave her some more warm clothes
25 and asked her to marry him.

*   *   *

Meanwhile, the other six sisters were back in heaven. Their grandmother, the Queen of Heaven, was very upset. She loved her granddaughter and was worried about her. She was also

very angry, because this lost granddaughter
30 was very clever. She was able to weave the most beautiful cloth, and so people called her Weaving Girl. Everyone wanted the material she wove.

The Queen of Heaven said, "I hope that
35 Weaving Girl is happy. I miss her terribly. And I will miss the beautiful material she makes."

The six sisters felt sad. They missed Weaving Girl too. Was she safe? Was she
40 happy?

*   *   *

Weaving Girl was very safe and very happy. She loved her husband and the cowherd loved her. She was a mother now: first she had a baby boy, then she had a baby girl. Three years passed very quickly. But then everything changed. The Queen
45 of Heaven wanted some fine cloth, and nobody in heaven could weave it.

The Queen of Heaven said to a servant, "Nobody can make cloth like my granddaughter. Bring Weaving Girl back to heaven."
50 Weaving Girl did not want to leave earth, but everyone obeyed the Queen of Heaven. One moment Weaving Girl was with her babies, and the next moment she was back with her six sisters. Her husband and babies were still on earth.

"Please let me go back," she begged, but her grandmother,
55 the Queen of Heaven, replied, "I need you here, my child. I want you to weave for me."

The cowherd was left on earth, sad and alone. He grieved for his wife and at last his heart broke. He died and went into the sky.

60 The Queen of Heaven did not want the cowherd to find Weaving Girl. She took her magic hairpin from her hair and drew thousands of stars in the sky. The cowherd could not cross the
65 silver stream of heaven. Weaving Girl was on one side, and the cowherd on the other. They were unable to speak to each other, and unable to touch . . . .

70 And so it is, every day of the year. If you look up at the Milky Way, you can see their stars. Weaving Girl is on one side of the Milky Way, and the Cowherd on the other. Every day, that is, but one. On the seventh day of the seventh moon, all
75 the blackbirds in the world fly up to make a bridge, and the lovers cross the bridge to be together.

Are You Listening?

Look at page 80. Find the words "Meanwhile, the other six sisters were back in heaven" on line 26. Your teacher will read this part of the story. You read the book and listen. When you hear something different from the book, say "Excuse me" and tell your teacher what the book really says.

Example: Excuse me. The book says "six," not "seven."

What Did You Understand?

A. Underline the correct words. Follow the example.

Once upon a time the (six   <u>seven</u>   eight) granddaughters of the Queen of Heaven were swimming. A young (farmer   woodcutter   cowherd) saw them, and stole the clothes that belonged to the (youngest   middle   eldest) sister, Weaving Girl. Weaving Girl stayed on earth and married the cowherd. They were very happy together, and they had two children.

The Queen of Heaven wanted some fine (food   cloth   birds). She brought Weaving Girl back to heaven. Then she made some stars into a (stream   road   wall) of light. The cowherd and Weaving Girl can only be together on the seventh day of the seventh moon, when the (sisters   birds   stars) make a bridge across the stream of light.

B. Number these events in the correct order. Follow the example.

____ The youngest sister married the cowherd.

____ The Queen of Heaven made a stream of stars to keep the lovers apart.

____ Weaving Girl and the cowherd cross a bridge of blackbirds and meet once a year.

_1_ The seven sisters swam in a pond.

____ The cowherd stole the clothes of the youngest sister.

____ The Queen of Heaven brought Weaving Girl back to heaven.

Show What It Means

Work with a partner. Answer these questions.

1. Who lost something in the story? Point to the line number where you find the answer.

2. What did this person lose?   What happened as a result?

Now show how you look when you have lost something valuable, like a key or a passport.

How do you feel? Choose from these words and phrases.

| a little bit sick | frightened | happy | sad | very worried |

Work with Words

A. **Work with a partner. Complete the sentences with the words in the box. Follow the example.**

sister

hut

weave

hairpin

bridge

shelter

1. When you _W_ _e_ _a_ _v_ _e_ you make threads into a material.

2. If it is windy and rainy, we need to find __ __ __ __ __ __ __ .

3. People sometimes hold long hair in place with a
__ __ __ __ __ __ __ .

4. Do you have a brother or a __ __ __ __ __ __ ?

5. A very small, very simple house is a __ __ __ .

6. Sometimes there is a __ __ __ __ __ __ across a river.

B. **Guess the meanings of the underlined words and phrases. If you need help, look at the other sentences around them in the story. Circle the letter of the correct answer.**

1. They played in the water, and laughed, and <u>splashed each other</u>.   (line 5)

    a. threw water on each other

    b. shouted at each other

    c. laughed at each other

2. Their youngest sister was left alone, <u>weeping bitterly</u>.   (line 20)

    a. enjoying herself

    b. crying very sadly

    c. crying a little

3. <u>Meanwhile</u>, the other six sisters were back in heaven.   (line 26)

    a. at the same time

    b. years and years later

    c. the day before

4. Their grandmother, the Queen of Heaven, was <u>very upset</u>.   (line 27)

    a. pleased

    b. sleeping

    c. worried and angry

5. He <u>grieved for his wife</u> and at last his heart broke.   (lines 57–58)

    a. felt sorry for his wife

    b. felt very sad about his wife

    c. was not upset about his wife

How Do You Sound?

How do people sound when they really want something?

"Please let me go back," she begged. . . .

In English, asking for things you really want is called *begging*, or *pleading*.

Take turns. Read these sentences to a partner. Then your partner will read them to you. Try to sound like you are begging or pleading.

1. Please, may I have a pencil?

2. Please pass the salt.

3. Please let me through.

4. Please give me a chance.

5. Please sit down in this chair.

6. Please give it to me.

Now say the same sentences again, like normal requests.

What Happened?

Write the correct answers. Follow the example.

1. Was Weaving Girl unhappy with the cowherd, or was she happy?

   Weaving Girl was happy with the cowherd.

2. Did Weaving Girl give the cowherd her clothes, or did he steal them?

   _____

3. Did the Queen of Heaven want Weaving Girl back because she loved her, or because she made such good material?

   _____

4. Was the cowherd a good husband, or was he cruel to his wife?

_____

5. Do the blackbirds make a bridge every day, or one day a year?

_____

Tic Tac Toe

Divide into two teams, the X team and the O team. Play a game of tic tac toe on the chalkboard. The first team to get three Xs or Os in a row wins.

Now play tic tac toe with words. To win a square, a team member must say the word opposite in meaning to the word in the square he or she has chosen. If the other team says it is not the correct word, and your teacher agrees, they get a chance to say the correct word and win the square.

QUICKLY	YOUNGEST	SISTER
SMALL	LONG	SAD
OPEN	WIFE	QUEEN

E X P A N D a Sentence

Work in groups of three. Make each sentence bigger. Add one word at a time.

Example:

The kind blackbirds made a bridge.
The kind blackbirds quickly made a bridge.
The kind blackbirds quickly made a beautiful bridge.

Here are some words you can use. You don't have to use them all, and you may use words that are not on this list.

old	angry	very	fairy	beautiful	pretty	six
lightly	quickly	up	unhappy	poor	broken-hearted	
kind	happily	soon				

1. The cowherd stole the clothes.

2. The sisters flew to heaven.

3. The Queen of Heaven was angry.

4. The cowherd died.

Describe the Picture

Work with a partner. Describe what is happening in the last picture on page 79.

Here are some questions to help you.

What are the birds doing?

Why?

How does the cowherd feel?

How does Weaving Girl feel?

Do you like the picture? Why? Why not?

What Do You Think?

Would you like the Queen of Heaven for your grandmother? Why? Why not? Talk in groups of three. Be ready to share your answer with the class.

Beyond the Story

This is the end of the story about Weaving Girl and the cowherd.

"On the seventh day of the seventh moon, all the blackbirds in the world fly up to make a bridge, and the lovers cross the bridge to be together."

In the Western calendar people divide the year into 12 months. Do you know what their names are? In the lunar calendar people divide the year into 12 moons. A new moon means a new month. The new year begins on the day of the new moon at the end of January or beginning of February.

A moon is about 29 1/2 days long. The seventh day of the seventh moon is around September 20.

Here's a poem that tells how many days there are in the months.

> Thirty days hath* September
> April, June and November
> All the rest have thirty-one
> Excepting February alone
> Which has but twenty-eight days clear,
> And twenty-nine in a Leap Year.

* "Hath" is an old word for "has."

How is the year divided in your culture? When is the new year? Draw a calendar from your country or bring one in to show the class.

Teacher's Notes

Please read the Introduction on pages iv–vi.

The Eagle and the Snake

BEFORE YOU READ

4. You could ask "Has there ever been fighting in your country? Why?" if appropriate for your class.

ARE YOU LISTENING?

Read the following passage to the students. Changes from the original are in bold-face; the original words are in parentheses. You read the boldface word, e.g., "'This is a pretty place,' they said."

*"This is a **pretty** (wonderful) place," they said. "Maybe the eagle is here." They waited for the **bird** (eagle), but it did not come.*

*The priests said, "We cannot **build our city** (stay) here. We will go on." So the people **walked** (traveled) on.*

*"I want to find the eagle soon," a **child** (woman) said. She sounded very tired. Everyone agreed with her. They wanted to **see** (find) the eagle, too. They kept on walking. They hoped the land of the eagle was **close** (not too far away).*

*At last the **people** (Aztecs) came to a beautiful place. It was a small strip of land next to a pretty lake. The **Aztec** (Toltec) people who lived there were angry. They tried to drive the Aztecs away.*

*The Aztecs fought **gently** (bravely). There were many fierce battles. **Then** (At last) the Aztecs won.*

Read slowly and be careful not to change inflection before you read the changes. Encourage students to interrupt you politely and to correct the sentences using appropriate language and intonation.

WHAT DID YOU UNDERSTAND?

A. Long ago, walked, north, tired, snake, lake

B. The best summary is 3. If you have some more advanced students, ask them why the summary they chose is the best one. Encourage students to justify their choice.

SHOW WHAT IT MEANS

1. the people (line 7), a woman (line 29)

2. They were tired because they had walked a long way.

Although this is a scanning exercise, there is no need to hurry students at this level.

Check that students' body language, facial expressions, and mimes are appropriate. If there is time, you may want to repeat the exercise with three adjectives: energetic, tired, exhausted.

WORK WITH WORDS

A. 1. eagle 2. Tired 3. safe 4. bravely 5. overhead 6. journey

B. 1. city 2. eagle 3. build 4. mountains 5. tired 6. Aztecs. Encourage students to explain their choices.

SEPARATETHEWORDS. SEPARATE/THE/WORDS.

After students have separated the words, write the sentences on the board as they dictate. Ask the students for help spelling homophones, e.g., "How do you spell 'to'? 't-o' or 't-w-o'?"

NORTH, SOUTH, EAST, WEST

Let students refer to the world map on page 1 while they play this game.

HOW DO YOU SOUND?

Students who speak tonal languages like Chinese use a narrower band of intonation than do English speakers. Encourage students from these language backgrounds to exaggerate their inflection, but don't insist if they seem uncomfortable.

WHAT HAPPENED?

A. 1. The Aztecs walked for a long time.
   2. The priests told the Aztecs to look for an eagle eating a snake.
   3. The Toltecs fought with the Aztecs.
   4. The Aztecs built a city by the lake.

B. After students have compared their sentences with partners, elicit answers from the class to write a master list on the board.

BEYOND THE STORY

You may want to assign this activity as homework. Ask students to bring in books or pictures to help them talk about their flag.

If you have any pictures or books related to Mexico, bring them in to share with the students.

Bouki Rents a Horse

BEFORE YOU READ

6. b. Distinguish between the meanings of *buy* (a), *rent* (b), and *borrow* (c).

ARE YOU LISTENING?

Read the following passage to the students. Changes from the original are in bold-face, the original words are in parentheses. You read the boldface word, e.g., "Bouki had a lot of yams in his house."

*Bouki had a lot of yams in his **house** (garden). He dug them up and made a pile. It was time to take them to **the kitchen** (market).*

*Bouki looked at the big pile of **apples** (yams). There were far too many for **them** (him) to carry! "I want a **cart** (horse) or a donkey," Bouki **thought** (said). He went to see his friend Moussa.*

*"Moussa," he asked, "can I **take** (borrow) your donkey?"*

*Moussa looked sad and worried. "My donkey is not here," he said. "I can't find him anywhere. Ask Toussaint to **give** (lend) you his horse."*

*"Ask Toussaint!" Bouki said. "That's a **good** (bad) idea. Toussaint's so greedy! He wants **dollars** (money) for everything."*

WHAT DID YOU UNDERSTAND?

A. yams, borrow, greedy, money, angry, fifteen

B. 5, 1, 3, 4, 2

SHOW WHAT IT MEANS

1. Sad: Moussa (line 10), Bouki (line 28).
2. Worried: Moussa (line 10), Toussaint (line 59).
3. Angry: Toussaint (line 75).
4. Happy: Moussa (line 30).

Check that student's body language, facial expressions, and mimes are appropriate. If there is time, repeat the exercise with the continuum of not very sad, sad, and very sad.

WORK WITH WORDS

A. 1. yams 2. middle 3. yell 4. money 5. laugh 6. greedy

B.

WOMEN	MEN
Mother	*Father*
Daughter	*Son*
Grandmother	Grandfather
Aunt	Uncle
Granddaughter	*Grandson*
Sister	*Brother*
Niece	*Nephew*
Cousin	*Cousin*

SEPARATETHEWORDS. SEPARATE/THE/WORDS.

After students have separated the words, write the sentences on the board as they dictate. Ask the students for help with spelling, and be sure to have the students repeat if they do not speak clearly.

ACT LIKE YOU FEEL

Suggested instructions: Be prepared to demonstrate the action.

You are angry: Stamp your feet. Make a fist. Frown. Look happy. Smile. Laugh.
You are sad: Laugh. Cry. Look unhappy. Look happy. Smile.
You are happy: Laugh. Smile. Frown. Stamp your foot. Look sad. Look happy.

HOW DO YOU SOUND?

Read lines 75–78: *"Here!" Toussaint said angrily. "Take the fifteen dollars!" He gave Bouki ten more dollars. "Now give me my horse!" And he jumped on the horse's back and rode away.* Exaggerate the angry intonation. Encourage students to repeat Toussaint's words using appropriate intonation.

CONNECT THE SENTENCES

1. e 2. d 3. a 4. b 5. c.

WHAT HAPPENED?

1. Bouki paid money for the horse.

2. Bouki rented a horse from Toussaint.

3. Toussaint took his horse away.

4. Toussaint was angry at the end of the story.

DESCRIBING PEOPLE

	BOUKI	TI MALICE	TOUSSAINT
clever		✓	
worried			✓
angry			✓
greedy			✓
silly	✓		

Encourage students to explain why they chose the characteristics of each person.

MAKE IT TRUE

1. Bouki was not a very clever man.

2. Toussaint did not want a lot of people to sit on the horse.

3. Toussaint gave Bouki fifteen dollars.

4. A big horse cannot carry ten people on its back.

BEYOND THE STORY

Ask students to tell the class about their fruits and vegetables, using visuals if possible.

If you have pictures or books related to Haiti, bring them in to share with the students.

Anansi and the Stories

Anansi is the spider hero of many West Indian folktales. He originated in Ghana as the Ashanti Spider God. His main attribute is always his cleverness. In other tales he changes from spider to man.

ARE YOU LISTENING?

Read the following passage to the students. Changes from the original are in bold-face; the original words are in parentheses. You read the boldface word, e.g., "'Good evening, Tiger,' Anansi said."

"Good evening, **Tiger** (Snake)," Anansi said. "I'm sorry you are not the longest thing in the forest anymore."

"What **are you saying** (do you mean)?" Snake asked.

"Tiger says the **tree** (bamboo) is longer," Anansi said. "See? Here is a long **stick** (piece) of bamboo. I'm sure it's longer than you are."

Snake **growled** (sniffed). "We'll soon see about that!" he said. He wound himself around the bamboo. Anansi ran up and down the **branch** (bamboo).

"I can't see which is longer," **Snake** (Anansi) said. "I think you are moving up the bamboo."

"I'm not moving," Snake **yelled** (said).

"Maybe not," Anansi said, "but I can't say for sure that you are longer than the bamboo. Too **bad** (Sorry)." Anansi turned away.

"I know," said Snake. "Tie my **head** (tail) to the bamboo. Then you know I can't move."

Anansi came back. "All right," he said. "**Maybe** (Perhaps) that will help." So he tied Snake's tail to the bamboo. Then he ran up to Snake's **tail** (head).

"You're almost here!" Anansi said. "Stretch, **Tiger** (Snake), stretch!"

WHAT DID YOU UNDERSTAND?

A. small, Tiger, catch, escaped, jungle, bamboo

B. The best summary is 2, which is complete and accurate. If you have some more advanced students, ask them why the summary they chose is the best one. Encourage students to justify their choice.

DESCRIBE THE PICTURE

Snake is very long. He is twisted around a piece of bamboo. Anansi is talking to Tiger. Tiger's mouth is closed. He looks a little surprised. The other animals are watching.

WORK WITH WORDS

A. 1. bamboo 2. stories 3. tie 4. trap 5. escaped 6. clever

B.

TIGER	ANANSI
big	_small_
brave	timid
proud	humble
powerful	_weak_

Possible answers for Anansi are: clever, smart, funny.
Possible answers for Tiger are: frightening, mean, angry, fierce.

ANANSI SAYS

Suggested actions: Stand up, sit down, stretch your arms, touch your desk/table, touch your face, stick out your tongue, touch your ear, touch your knee, smile, growl, laugh, look up/down/sideways, draw in your breath, look out the window, look through the door, look at the ceiling, look at the floor.

HOW DO YOU SOUND?

Be lenient in your judgments here. Students should see that there can be emphasis in a sentence and that change in emphasis can change meaning. If they grasp this concept quickly, try changing the emphasis and see if they understand how the meaning has changed: *My* friend was at that table (not your friend). My friend *was* at that table (it's true my friend was there OR my friend is no longer there). My friend was at *that* table (and no other). My friend was at that *table* (not any other piece of furniture). These are fairly sophisticated distinctions, but students begin to understand them at this level.

WHAT HAPPENED?

1. Anansi had to try again.
2. Anansi tricked Snake.
3. Tiger gave the stories to Anansi.
4. Tiger was angry at the end of the story.

SUMMARIZE THE STORY

Anansi asked Tiger for the stories. Tiger told Anansi to catch Snake. Anansi showed Snake a piece of bamboo. Anansi was very clever and tricked Snake. Tiger gave Anansi the stories.

BEYOND THE STORY

Set aside time for a story hour, and have students take turns telling stories from their native cultures. Encourage students to illustrate their stories. You may want to have them vote on which story they liked best.

If you have pictures or books related to Jamaica, bring them in to share with the students.

A Dinner of Smells

Stories about Nasrudin, the wise *mullah*, appear in many different places in the Middle East.

ARE YOU LISTENING?

Read the following passage to the students. Changes from the original are in boldface; the original words are in parentheses. You read the boldface word, e.g., "Nasrudin stepped backward."

*Nasrudin stepped **backward** (forward). "This man is my friend," he said. "Can I pay for **her** (him)?" He held out a bag of **chocolates** (money).*

*The judge looked at the **shop** (restaurant) owner. "Can Nasrudin pay?" he asked.*

*"Yes," the restaurant owner said. "Nasrudin has **many camels** (money). The poor man does not. Nasrudin can pay!"*

*Nasrudin **laughed** (smiled). He stood next to the restaurant owner.*

*Nasrudin held the bag of money near the restaurant owner's **foot** (ear). He moved it around so the **stones** (coins) made a noise.*

WHAT DID YOU UNDERSTAND?

A. poor, smelling, owner, stealing, wise, listen to

B. 5, 3, 2, 6, 4, 1

SHOW WHAT IT MEANS

Check that the students' body language, facial expressions, and mimes are appropriate.

WORK WITH WORDS

1. payment 2. restaurant 3. delicious 4. wise 5. owner 6. hungry

HOW DO YOU SOUND?

Encourage students to exaggerate their inflections.

TIC TAC TOE

Play several games of conventional tic tac toe with students before playing this game of "opposite" tic tac toe.

WHAT HAPPENED?

A. 1. The poor man was still very hungry.

2. Nasrudin was a wise man.

3. The judge was a friend of the restaurant owner.

4. The restaurant owner was a cruel man.

5. Nasrudin let the restaurant owner hear the money.

B. Answers will vary. Accept any answer which conveys that:

1. The restaurant owner took the poor man to court for smelling his food.

2. Nasrudin did not give the judge any money. He did not give the restaurant owner any money either. He let the restaurant owner hear the sound of money in a bag.

EXPAND A SENTENCE

Divide the class into groups of three. Have the groups write their sentences on the chalkboard. If necessary, write the following example on the chalkboard: The dog ran. The fat dog ran. The fat brown dog ran. The old fat brown dog ran. The old fat brown dog ran quickly. The old fat brown dog ran very quickly.

DESCRIBING THINGS

After the students have written their food-related words, elicit a list to write on the chalkboard. Have them use some of the words to write a description of a meal from their native countries. The model provided will help them structure their descriptions.

BEYOND THE STORY

Have students tell the class about the pictures they bring in. You may want to set aside time for a food fair and have the class bring or prepare some of their favorite dishes.

If you have pictures or books related to the Middle East, bring them in to share with the students.

The Blue Lady of Jagua Castle

ARE YOU LISTENING?

Read the following passage to the students. Changes from the original are in boldface; the original words are in parentheses. You read the boldface word, e. g., "One morning a new young man was in Jagua Castle."

*One morning a new young **man** (soldier) was in Jagua Castle. It was his first day in the army.*

*"Did the **other people** (soldiers) tell you about the Blue Lady?" a sergeant asked the new man.*

*"I don't think so," the **new** (young) soldier answered.*

*"They never tell new men about the **young** (Blue) Lady," the sergeant said. "They're afraid that they'll run **off** (away)." He looked at the young soldier. "Don't go out on a **sunny** (moonlit) night," he said. "That's when she walks. You don't believe me, do you? I tell you, when the moon comes out, the Blue Lady walks."*

*"What does she look like?" the young man **said to** (asked) the sergeant. "What does she do?"*

*"Nobody goes **next** (close) to her," the sergeant said **loudly** (softly). "All you see is a woman in blue. Her dress is long. She has a blue scarf over her head, so you can't see her **head** (face). She walks outside the castle in the moonlight. She crosses the terrace, very slowly and quietly. She **walks** (moves) gracefully, the way a beautiful woman walks. I think she was a great lady."*

Now read lines 57–65 in a haunted, spooky voice. Encourage students to volunteer their opinions about what makes the story frightening.

WHAT DID YOU UNDERSTAND?

A. ghost, woman, moon, lieutenant, morning, skeleton

B. 3, 5, 1, 4, 6, 2

SHOW WHAT IT MEANS

A. 1. the soldiers (lines 31–37), the lieutenant (lines 57–58)

    2. The sergeant was afraid of the ghost, and telling the story makes him remember being afraid. The lieutenant was afraid of the ghost.

B. Some possible answers:

We are worried about the lieutenant.

The teacher's voice makes the story frightening.

The lieutenant sounds very alone.

It's frightening when the air changes from being warm to cold.

Although this is a scanning exercise, there is no need to hurry students at this level.

WORK WITH WORDS

1. forbid 2. night 3. alone 4. old 5. morning 6. cold

DESCRIBE THE PICTURE

The lieutenant is lying on the castle terrace very close to a skeleton. He is looking away from the skeleton. The skeleton is wearing the same long dark blue gown as the Blue Lady. We can see her skull. It's morning.

GIVING ORDERS AND MAKING REQUESTS

Be sure the students understand the difference between an order and a request, and use an appropriately polite tone when making a request.

WHAT HAPPENED?

1. The lieutenant was a brave man.

2. The sergeant tried to frighten the young soldier.

3. The sergeant believed the story.

4. I think the Blue Lady really came. OR I think it is just a story.

WHAT DO YOU THINK?

After the students have written their classmates' ideas, you may want to write some of them on the chalkboard. Some possibilities are: He didn't want the story to frighten the soldiers. He thought it was silly. He didn't believe in the Blue Lady.

BEYOND THE STORY

The storytelling may be best done in groups of about five students.

If you have any pictures or books related to Cuba, bring them in to share with the students.

The Monkey's Heart

BEFORE YOU READ

A. 1. b   2. c   3. d   4. a   5. f   6. e

ARE YOU LISTENING?

Read the following passage to the students. Changes from the original are in bold-face; the original words are in parentheses. You read the boldface word, e.g., "'Monkey,' the crocodile said, 'why do you **buy** figs?'"

*"Monkey," the crocodile said, "why do you **buy** (eat) figs? On the other side of the river there are **apples** (bananas). They are large and sweet as **you are** (honey)."*

The monkey loved to eat bananas.

*"I know about those bananas," the **crocodile** (monkey) said sadly. "I will never eat them, because they're on the other side of the river. And alas! There's no **road** (bridge). The water is deep and it moves **slowly** (quickly). I cannot swim, so I can never go to the other side."*

*The crocodile **smiled** (laughed). "Of course you can!" he said. "Get on my back. I'll take you across the river."*

*The monkey jumped onto the crocodile's back, and the crocodile swam into the middle of the **road** (river). Then the crocodile said, "I'm going to **eat** (kill) you."*

*The monkey was very frightened. "Why are you going to kill me?" he asked. "I'm only a **little** (thin) monkey. I'm not fat enough to eat."*

*"I want your **head** (heart)," the crocodile replied. "When I have your heart, I'll be able to **play** (swing) in the trees, just like you do."*

WHAT DID YOU UNDERSTAND?

A. swing, heart, swim, river, fig tree, gray

B. 1. F The crocodile wanted the monkey's heart.

2. T

3. F The crocodile hid in the river and made his plans.

4. F The crocodile pretended to be a big gray log.

5. T

SHOW WHAT IT MEANS

The monkey moved lightly (line 3).

These activities can be done with hand movements if you don't want students to move around the classroom.

WORK WITH WORDS

A. 1. log   2. monkey   3. heart   4. swim   5. banana   6. swing

B. 1. tree   2. fish   3. bridge   4. dry   5. land   6. reply

HOW DO YOU SOUND?

Be sure students distinguish between the way people speak when praising (or "selling") something and the way they speak when skeptical or disdainful.

WHAT HAPPENED?

1. The story happened in India.

2. The monkey was clever.

3. Monkeys are good at swinging through the trees.

4. The crocodile wanted the monkey's heart.

BEYOND THE STORY

You may want students to prepare their presentations as homework. Ask them to bring in books and pictures to help them talk about their animals. If you have any pictures or books related to India, bring them in to share with the students.

The Moon God of the Mayas

ARE YOU LISTENING?

Read the following passage to the students. Changes from the original are in boldface; the original words are in parentheses. You read the boldface word, e.g., "One morning the Moon God went back as usual."

*One morning the Moon God went **back** (home) as usual. He was tired, and very ready to go to bed and **rest** (sleep), but something was wrong. There was a small green turtle **sitting** (lying) on his bed!*

"What are you doing here?" the Moon God asked. "This is a very small bed. There isn't enough room for both of us."

*The Moon God was very tired, so he **helped** (threw) the little turtle out of the cave. Soon he was **awake** (asleep).*

*The next night the Moon God got up and **went** (walked) across the sky as usual. When he came **back** (home) he looked at his bed. There was a medium-sized turtle lying in it.*

*"Get out!" the Moon God **said** (yelled). "I want to go to sleep." He threw the turtle out of the cave. It was more **easy** (difficult) to move this turtle, because it was bigger.*

*The next morning the Moon God hurried home. He wanted to see if there was another turtle in his **house** (bed).*

*This time, the turtle was very big. It took the Moon God a long time to **carry** (drag) it out of the bed. He was very angry, and it was hard for him to sleep.*

"I can't live like this," the Moon God said to himself. He went to see his friend the Water God.

WHAT DID YOU UNDERSTAND?

A. green, morning, another turtle, guard, himself, sky
B. 1. T   2. F   3.T   4. T

SHOW WHAT IT MEANS

The Moon God was tired because he walked across the sky (line 10).

Check that students' body language, facial expressions, and mimes are appropriate.

WORK WITH WORDS

A. 1. turtle   2. medium   3. cave   4. rain   5. bed   6. threw

B. Write the students' sentences on the chalkboard.

HOW DO YOU SOUND?

Encourage the students to exaggerate the difference between sounding tired and sounding alert.

WHAT HAPPENED?

1. The Moon God was angry to see the turtles.
2. The Water God helped the Moon God.
3. The Moon God stayed in his own cave.
4. The Moon God kept the turtles away.
5. The Moon God found a way to be in two places at the same time.

FIND THE STORY

Encourage students to explain how they made their choices.

The Moon God was very angry about green turtles. He found them in his bed. At first it was not so bad, because the turtle was little and easy to throw out of the cave. The next time, however, the turtle was larger. The Moon God decided never to let a turtle into his cave again. Now he leaves part of himself in the cave to keep the turtles away.

BEYOND THE STORY

After students have talked to each other and completed their charts, ask them what they discovered. Korean students may see a hare or a brother and sister in the moon. Vietnamese students may see a little boy with a tree. Chinese students may see a toad, or a man trying to chop down a tree.

If you have any pictures or books related to the Mayan culture of Central America, bring them in to share with the students.

Pedro Animala Sells a Carrao Bird

ARE YOU LISTENING?

Read the following passage to the students. Changes from the original are in bold-face; the original words are in parentheses. You read the boldface word, e.g., "He lived long ago in the hills of Puerto Rico."

*There once was a trickster called Pedro Animala. He lived long ago in the **hills** (mountains) of Puerto Rico. He did not have a rich **business** (family), and he never **stayed** (worked) at a job. How did he earn money? He lived by **helping** (tricking) people.*

*One day Pedro trapped a young carrao bird. "What good luck," he thought. "Now I can **eat** (sell) it." So off to town he went, whistling happily as he walked.*

*On his way to town Pedro passed a neat, little **building** (house). He could see a woman inside the house. She was carefully putting papaya candy on a **bowl** (plate). He walked closer to the window and heard her say, "How happy my **friend** (husband) will be! I'll hide this candy and we'll eat it after dinner tonight! I'll hide it quickly, before he comes home." Pedro looked through the window and saw the woman put the plate at the very **front** (back) of the cupboard.*

Pedro hurried back to the road. He had an idea . . .

*Pedro held the carrao bird firmly under his arm and **walked** (marched) up to the woman's front door.*

WHAT DID YOU UNDERSTAND?

A. trickster, home, bird, bought, Soon, silly

B. 1. Pedro Animala trapped a carrao bird.
   2. Pedro did not understand what the bird was saying.
   3. T
   4. Pedro Animala tricked the woman.

SHOW WHAT IT MEANS

The woman feels sick because Pedro Animala tricked her (line 68). Check that the students' body language, facial expressions, and mimes are appropriate.

WORK WITH WORDS

1. silly   2. canary   3. curious   4. busy   5. trickster
6. future   7. march

CHANGE THE STORY

Be lenient about grammar in this game.

WHAT HAPPENED?

A. 1. Pedro Animala was a trickster.
   2. Pedro pretended to understand what the bird was saying.
   3. The woman in the story believed everything Pedro told her.
   4. Pedro Animala tricked a lot of people.
   5. The carrao bird could only say its name.

B. 1. Any reasonable answer, either physical or verbal, that shows that the students understand the determined nature of marching.
   2. Any reasonable answer that shows students understand the woman didn't want Pedro to realize she wanted the bird.
   3. Any reasonable answer that shows that Pedro, having committed his deception, wants to escape.
   4. Any reasonable answer that conveys that Pedro doesn't want to be recognized.

SCRAMBLED SENTENCES

1. Pedro wanted to sell a bird.
2. Pedro tricked the woman.
3. Pedro was very happy.
4. The woman tapped the bird on the head.
5. The husband came home and found his wife listening to the bird.

ASK THE CLASS

Have each student get opinions from three or four classmates. Then get the students to report on what their classmates said.

BEYOND THE STORY

Encourage students to use their imaginations in this role-playing.

If you have any pictures or books related to Puerto Rico, bring them in to share with the students.

Truong-Chi and the Princess

ARE YOU LISTENING?

Read the following passage to the students. Changes from the original are in bold-face; the original words are in parentheses. You read the boldface word, e.g., "'Who is this fellow?'"

*The king said to his servants, "Who is this **fellow** (man)? His song has made my daughter well again. Go and bring **the man** (him) to me."*

*The people at the **house** (palace) went out to find the boatman. They brought him back to the king.*

*The king sent a servant to find **the princess** (his daughter). "Your father found the boatman with the **lovely** (sweet) voice," the servant said. "His name is Truong-Chi. He's with your father now. Your father says the boatman is a fine man."*

*Quickly the princess put on her **oldest** (finest) clothes. Then she ran **upstairs** (downstairs). The boatman was talking to her **brother** (father). His back looked strong. The princess heard her heart beating **quietly** (loudly). Could the boatman hear it too?*

*The boatman turned around and bowed. The princess held her breath. Was he **beautiful** (handsome)? Then she saw his face, and she was so **surprised** (shocked) she felt sick. This was not the man of her dreams! This man's face was ordinary and ugly. The **king** (princess) looked away. She was a young girl, and saw only what people looked like. She had no idea if they were good or bad, kind or cruel.*

*"Come, my dear," the king said, but the **boatman** (princess) turned and ran from the room.*

WHAT DID YOU UNDERSTAND?

A. Vietnam, fell in love with, sick, song, palace, ran away, goblet, disappeared

B. 5, 3, 1, 4, 6, 2

WORK WITH WORDS

A. 1. servant   2. pale   3. window   4. alone   5. crystal
    6. handsome

B. PRINCESS: beautiful, truthful, cruel, sad, silly, unkind, waited patiently, lonely

   BOATMAN: kind, sad, strong, sang beautifully, ugly

Encourage students to give reasons for their answers. Accept any reasonable/ plausible answer.

THAT'S IN THE STORY!

If the students are finding this very easy, introduce a limit to the number of questions they may ask.

HOW DO YOU SOUND?

Be sure students' expressions of sadness and happiness are appropriate.

WHAT HAPPENED?

1. The princess was a silly, young girl.
2. The king liked the boatman.
3. The boatman loved the princess.
4. The crystal goblet was beautifully made.
5. The princess was not happy at the end of the story.
6. (Students can express an opinion or simply answer that the story makes them feel sad or happy.)

BEYOND THE STORY

Discuss the meaning of "Beauty is in the eye of the beholder." Ask students for similar expressions from their native languages and write the English translations on the chalkboard.

If you have any pictures or books related to Vietnam, bring them in to share with the students.

Weaving Girl and the Cowherd

ARE YOU LISTENING?

Read the following passage to the students. Changes from the original are in bold-face; the original words are in parentheses. You read the boldface word, e.g., "Meanwhile, the other seven sisters were back in heaven."

*Meanwhile, the other **seven** (six) sisters were back in heaven. Their grandmother, the Queen of Heaven, was very **happy** (upset). She loved her **grandson** (granddaughter) and was worried about her. She was also very angry, because this lost granddaughter was very **beautiful** (clever). She was able to **knit** (weave) the most beautiful cloth, and so **cowherds** (people) called her Weaving Girl. Everyone wanted the **things** (material) she wove.*

*The Queen of Heaven said, "I **know** (hope) that Weaving Girl is happy. I miss her **every day** (terribly). And I will miss the beautiful material she makes."*

*The six sisters felt **better** (sad). They missed Weaving Girl too. Was she safe? Was **he** (she) happy?*

WHAT DID YOU UNDERSTAND?

A. seven, cowherd, youngest, cloth, stream, birds

B. 3, 5, 6, 1, 2, 4

SHOW WHAT IT MEANS

1. Weaving Girl lost something in the story (lines 14–15).

2. She lost her clothes. As a result, she stayed on earth and married the cowherd.

Although this is a scanning exercise, there is no need to hurry students at this level.

WORK WITH WORDS

A. 1. weave   2. shelter   3. hairpin   4. sister   5. hut   6. bridge

B. 1. a   2. b   3. a   4. c   5. b

HOW DO YOU SOUND?

Listen to be sure students plead and request appropriately.

WHAT HAPPENED?

1. Weaving Girl was happy with the cowherd.
2. The cowherd stole Weaving Girl's clothes.
3. The Queen of Heaven wanted Weaving Girl back because she made such good material.
4. The cowherd was a good husband.
5. The blackbirds make a bridge one day a year.

TIC TAC TOE

Play several games of conventional tic tac toe with students before playing this game of "opposite" tic tac toe.

EXPAND A SENTENCE

Have students expand sentences in groups of three, then spot-check the expanded sentences on the chalkboard. Possible answers:

1. The lonely cowherd quickly stole the youngest sister's clothes.
2. The six beautiful fairy sisters flew lightly/quickly/happily up to heaven.
3. The sad, old Queen of Heaven was very angry.
4. The poor, kind, broken-hearted cowherd soon died.

BEYOND THE STORY

January, February, March, April, May, June, July, August, September, October, November, December.

If the students are in culturally diverse groups, get them to write a summary or chart of similarities and differences among their cultures. This can be transferred to the chalkboard.

If you have any pictures or books related to China, bring them in to share with the students.

Selected References

This is a list of some of the sources used in preparing this book. I am extremely grateful to the students who told me stories, or who added details to stories I had found elsewhere.

Campbell, Camilla. *Star Mountain and Other Mexican Legends*. New York: McGraw Hill, 1946.

Courlander, Harold. *The Piece of Fire and Other Haitian Tales.* New York: Harcourt, Brace & World, 1964.

Dobie, J. Frank. *Tongues of the Monte.* Austin: Univ. of Texas Press, 1980.

Fernandez, José B. *Los abuelos: Historia oral cubana.* Miami: Ediciones Universal 1987.

Guerber, H.A. *The Myths of Greece and Rome.* London: Harrap, 1938.

Khattab, Huda. *Stories from the Muslim World.* London: Macdonald, 1987.

Law, Joan, and Barbara E. Ward. *Chinese Festivals.* Hong Kong: South China Morning Post, Publications Division, 1982.

Lindstromberg, Seth, ed. *The Recipe Book.* White Plains, N.Y.: Longman, 1990.

Los Angeles Unified School District, Language Acquisition and Bilingual Development Branch. *English as a Second Language, Beginning ESL.* September 1992. Publication No. SC-982.

Los Angeles Unified School District, Office of Instruction Publication. *Secondary Teacher Handbook: Strategies for Teaching Limited-English-Proficient Students Grades Six through Twelve English–Language Arts.* 1992. Publication No. SC–984.4.

Marriott, Alice, and Carol K. Rachlin. *American Indian Mythology.* New York: Thomas Y. Crowell, 1968.

Milburn, Douglas. "The Story of Truong-Chi." *Houston City Magazine,* February 1984, 29.

Mohyeddin, Zia. *The Fables of India*. Caedman CDL–51168, audiocassettes.

Pollard, Velma. *Anansenem.* Longman: 1985.

Sherlock, Philip. *West Indian Folk Tales.* Oxford University Press: 1966.

7